The *Butterfly*

Man

A Memoir by
Brian House

RRP International Publishing LLC
Lexington, Ky.

RRP International LLC, DBA Eugenia Ruth LLC
838 E. High St.
Box #285
Lexington, Ky. 40502

www.rrpinternational.org

ISBN-13: 978-0-9971536-9-9

Dedication

To Susan, Sarah and Elliott. I love you always.

Table Of Contents

Introduction

I took a motorcycle ride across the country from Kentucky to New Mexico and back in June 2015. A lot of people take motorcycle trips every year so that in and of itself is no big deal. How I got there and why I did it? Well, that's been a big deal in my life. I was one kind of man before and another kind now who I'm still in the process of becoming. What that ride and the process of dealing with life leading up to it did for me has been monumental and I want to share it with you. I want you to see inside the transformative process of surviving the very bad news of a cancer diagnosis and the opportunity it provides to reorder your life and get on with it in a way that means there is a lot of good living ahead.

I should say at the outset that this book is not a "you have to go out and buy a motorcycle to have a life" piece. Far from it. It's about taking control of your life, recovering it when other things try to take it from you. It's about looking deep inside who you are at a given point in your life, who you wish you could be and taking steps to make it happen.

The title of this book is *The Butterfly Man*. I have been the caterpillar, lived in a cocoon of pain, suffering and transformation, and now I'm the Butterfly Man. There are too many caterpillars out there today and we need more butterflies. If this book helps some of you who read it see that you can, by act of will and with a lot of honesty, get to where you are the butterfly, then the writing of this book will have been worth it.

I hope you enjoy *The Butterfly Man*.

I'll see you on the road.

-Brian House

"Just when the caterpillar thought
The world was over
It became a butterfly"
-Unknown

Chapter 1

Caterpillar

I'm 57 years old as I write this. Back in 2012, I was 55 and things were looking up in my little world. I had been happily married for 33 years and was the father of two children, one adopted, the other biological. My children were successful in college and soon to get on with their careers. My daughter had survived a bout with thyroid cancer and her prognosis was excellent. My son was on the cusp of getting his undergraduate degree and entering graduate school. We had not incurred any debt to educate the children, so Susan and I were looking forward to what everyone told us would be some really good years as "empty nesters."

Empty nester is one of those code word phrases that people of a certain age throw around to let each other know they are in on the secret of getting just plain old. Rather than totally surrender to the concept that, yes, we too will someday end up in a retirement home eating watery oatmeal, we give little names to the steps along the way. I was OK with that. It did seem we would have some fun as we traveled and enjoyed some of that couple's time we had put on the back burner while raising our children.

I'm one of those dads who really liked raising his kids. I've never been a 19th hole guy or the type to hang out with my softball team. My crew was and is my family. The 19th holers are welcome to do whatever it is they do when they are leaving their wives and kids alone. I just preferred being with my family, whether it was hanging around the house, taking hikes, going to dance recitals or coaching their ball teams. Whatever it was, I liked being with my family. I was not one of those mid-50s men who had an agenda of things to do to flush the memories of raising my children down the tubes. I have always been active, done lots of things and incorporated those things into our family life. I simply wanted to keep living what had been a very good life, a safe life, an orderly life, a life with plans firmly made, money in the bank, a good career built upon years of hard work and one that should have gone on for years and years without having to face that dark precipice of impending death. I was in great health. I belonged to a local cycling club, had been a cyclist and runner for years and routinely rode 40 and 50 miles with ease. I rode centuries, 100-mile rides, several times a year on the bike as a measure, or perhaps a statement, of my fitness. For a man in his mid-50s, I was in good shape.

Part of taking care of yourself is, of course, going to the doctor and getting those annual check-ups to make sure things are all in order. When you are in really good health, it's almost an inconvenience to keep those appointments. I mean, why bother when you are more active than your doctor, right? That had been my attitude, but my wife Susan would insist I keep those appointments. I would set them on my birthday so I could make the annual check-up a thing I would not forget.

It always worked the same way. Susan and I would drive to Lexington, I would go to my little appointment and then we would go out to eat and celebrate my birthday and begin celebrating our wedding anniversary, which is the day after my birthday.

And so it was on August 19, 2012. My 55th birthday. A milestone of sorts, but really just another year. We drove to Lexington for my appointment with my urologist. Over the years I had suffered from an enlarged prostate and the accompanying infections. They preceded my years on the bike so it just seems to be something that was part of my physiology. It was an inconvenience, but I had learned to deal with it. I had kept regular appointments with my urologist in addition to my internist because of the prostate issues, but it was always routine.

Until August 19, 2012. Then routine went out the window.

For those of you who have no experience with men going to a urologist for prostate issues, the exam revolves around a digital exam where the physician inserts his finger into the patient's rectum and feels the prostate. An experienced urologist knows what to feel for. Healthy tissue should be resilient, soft and pliable. Infected tissue can be squishy or swollen. Cancerous tissue can be very hard. Hard is not a word you want to hear if you are a prostate patient.

"Gosh, that's really hard," said my urologist.

"What does that mean?"

"It means there's a 50 percent chance you have cancer. We'll watch it for a few months and then check again."

"OK. Whatever you say doctor."

It was not a great birthday celebration. I had to leave the doctor's office and tell my wife I had a 50 percent chance of having prostate cancer. Our dinner was subdued as I considered the news, or rather the 50 percent likelihood of bad news. My urologist wanted me to wait for six months and get checked again. This is what is called watchful waiting. I am not a watchful waiter. To me, either you have it or you don't. Find out and deal with it, but whatever you do, don't delay. Dealing with it and delaying do not go together well.

I thought about things overnight and then called my urologist and demanded a tissue biopsy immediately. He was not happy with me. He wanted to watch, but he said he would do it because I insisted. Two days later, I was at his office for the biopsy.

When you are trying to determine whether you have cancer, you can research things on the internet. You can talk to other people who have had similar problems arise. You can look at your PSA, that mysterious number that may or may not tell you something about prostate cancer. You can wait and test your number again and undergo another rectal exam. Sure, by all means do all of that and, by the way, it won't mean a thing. Only one thing can tell you whether you have cancer and that is a tissue biopsy where the tissue in question is removed from your body, placed under a microscope and viewed by a trained physician called a pathologist who will know if it is cancer by looking at it. A good pathologist can score the cancer and tell you what kind you have. This is important because there are many kinds of cancers, some more aggressive than others. As I learned, the experience of the pathologist also matters when it comes to reading the tissue samples.

The biopsy took less than four minutes and was performed by my urologist in his office. He gave me a shot to numb the rectal area and then proceeded to take some core samples with a needle biopsy device, basically a spring-fired hollow needle that inserts and retracts with tiny tissue samples. There was no bleeding for me. No pain. It was a minimally invasive procedure, but I've had teeth cleanings that hurt worse.

"I don't see anything to worry about. It looks good to me," says my urologist.

"Wonderful. Let me know when the results come in."

I walked out feeling good. If my doctor feels good, I can feel good.

A week later the call came.

"Well, it's a cancer and it's aggressive. You're going to have to deal with this," said my urologist who had been so encouraging only a week before.

"Let's cut it out and get rid of it." That had been my plan from the beginning. Go in and get the little bastard, kill it and throw it in a garbage can. I knew this was a strong possibility so I was ready to get it done.

"I'm not sure we can. It may be too late for you."

***　　　***　　　***　　　***　　　***

At that point my world as I knew it basically came to an end. Here I was in what I thought was the pinnacle of health for a middle-aged man. I had just been ordained as a minister in the Christian Church (Disciples of Christ) after years of seminary and my law practice was booming. These were supposed to be the really good years, right? Going to Paris and all that stuff. Trips to the Sonoma Valley drinking wine and eating cheese. Riding my bicycle to Prudhoe Bay, Alaska. Now all of that was out the window and my life along with it.

I make my living as a problem solver. That's what lawyers do. People come to us with things they can't resolve and we fix it for them. I wanted to do that with this prostate cancer, but there are times when it's best to step aside and ask others for help. You learn to do that with cancer. In fact, if you want to have any chance of living whatsoever, you get the hell out of the way quickly and let the people who know what they are doing take over and get to work saving your life. That is where Susan stepped in.

She was with me when I got the call. We were both confused and disappointed by the mixed signals we had received from my urologist during the diagnosis phase. I was not thinking clearly at this point. All I wanted was surgery and someone to tell me I was going to be ok. I did what I always do when I'm under pressure: I went back to work and kept helping others. Susan in the meantime, got on the phone and called my nephew, Dr. Alan Northington, an eminent radiologist in Louisville.

It pays to have brilliant nephews. It pays even more to have brilliant nephews who are physicians who care about you. Alan basically took charge of my life at that point. He had me at his facility in Louisville the next day where his partners ran the scans that would determine whether I would be eligible for surgery.

Most men think they can have surgery for prostate cancer if they ever have it and it will all be over. Not so. Before you can even consider surgery, the doctors must first determine whether the cancer has spread. There is another dreaded word in the cancer lexicon: Spread. Trust me, you do not want to hear that word. Here are the other words you don't want to hear in connection with spread: lymph nodes and bones. If the cancer has spread to either of these areas, you can't be cured. If it is in the nodes, you can be effectively treated and do have the chance of outliving the disease. If the cancer is already in your bones, then you had best get your affairs in order. How do I know this? My brilliant nephew, whom I love like my own son, was honest enough to tell me those things on that first morning as we sat there getting ready for the scans that would tell me whether I had a fighting chance or none at all.

I had two scans. The first was a CT scan of my abdomen. It would tell us whether the cancer could be illuminated just in the prostate area or if it appeared to have already spread. This is the first threshold test. You want the scan to just illuminate in the area of the prostate. They read this scan quickly, within an hour or so. I laid on the table and the machine scanned me and did its work. You learn early on in cancer treatment that machines do lots of the work. You learn to like machines and thank God for the men and women who invented them and who know how to use them.

I went out to the waiting room to find Susan and the two of us went to a little chapel in the hospital, praying and waiting. Being a minister, I would like to tell you I said all kinds of prayers and got things fixed quickly with God and that I had a clear message from Him that all was going to be fine. I could tell you that and none of it would be true. I basically just sat there petrified trying to figure out how to take care of my family if I got really bad news. I had the money taken care of, but not being there to help my family through life was something I had not planned on at 55.

We went back out to the waiting room and in a little while

Alan gave us the first good news. The scan showed the cancer just in the prostate. It had not illuminated anywhere else in my abdomen. So far so good.

Next came the whole body bone scan. This was really important. Prostate cancer is prostate cancer while it's in the prostate. Let it get into your bones and then it is just plain old badass cancer that is going to, with all certainty, kill your ass. You don't want to hear that news.

So, I drank some radioactive stuff and into the bone scan machine I went. As with a lot of cancer diagnostics and treatments, it is basically painless. The waiting will drive you crazy, but the scan was painless. The results from this scan would not be available for several hours. The radiologists had to read every square inch of the scans to see if they could find evidence of metastatic cancer in my bones. Susan and I opted to leave the facility and begin the two-and-a-half-hour drive back to our home. We would drive and wait for Alan to call at the same time.

The phone rang after we had been driving for about an hour. The cancer was not in my bones. This was the second good news, and it was really, really good. Now I had a fighting chance and I had always liked to fight. Now to find a good surgeon, and for that I again did what I would do over and over again in this journey: I turned to other people who knew more than I did and let them make the decision. Alan stepped in again.

I had done enough reading in those first early days to know robotic surgery was being performed with good results. The trick was to find a surgeon who had performed a lot of robotic procedures since the learning curve with the robot, known as the Da Vinci Robot, is very steep. Alan found me the most experienced surgeon in the area, Dr. Bradley Bell. From there on, Dr. Bell became an important figure in my life.

Alan scheduled me an early appointment with Dr. Bell and I was off into the world of cancer surgery and all that it entails. Susan and I met with Dr. Bell the next week. Things were moving fast. It was still not certain he would perform the surgery. The surgeon makes the decision about the benefit of surgery versus other types of treatment like radioactive seed implants or cryotherapy, which is freezing the cancerous tissue. I wanted the surgery so that if some remnant of cancer had gotten out of the prostate into surrounding tissue then I could radiate it and get rid of it. Dr. Bell would let me know whether I could undergo the surgery.

You will notice Susan was with me every step of the way. Prostate cancer is absolutely a couple's issue. What happens to the man during the treatment has a profound impact on the sexual relationship between the partners, and it is best for both to be informed from day one. Since cancer kills and prostate cancer is the second leading cause of death for men in America, it only made sense for Susan to be there so she would know everything I knew and, in truth, she knew more because she was listening with a clearer head than her husband the cancer patient. She and I have done a lot of sitting together in cancer doctors' offices since this all began.

Dr. Bell read my scans, biopsy and other medical records and explained to me I would be eligible for surgery, but it would have to be the most radical kind, what is called non-nerve sparing since the cancer had hit the nerve that runs through my prostate gland. This would make having sex difficult, but not impossible. I quite honestly could have cared less about sex at that point. My primary responsibility as a husband and a father was to be there for my family and the rest be damned.

"Well, Dr. Bell, you can gut me like a fish. Just keep me alive for my family. Let's get on with it."

It was an emotional moment. People get emotional over ball teams or political races. I could give a shit. I get emotional over trying to stay alive, over fighting to be here another day for my family. Tell me what I have to do in order to accomplish that goal and I'll do it.

Even Dr. Bell had tears in his eyes.

"Then we'll get you scheduled as soon as possible."

And with that I was on my way.

Surgery was scheduled for October 8, less than a month off which, in the world of prostate cancer surgery, is really fast. Most men wait four to six months for their surgery. I was very fortunate to get an early date. I later found out my date was possible because a man who had a much less aggressive tumor stepped aside for me to have my surgery. I'll never know who he was, but I am thankful for his kindness.

The month of waiting for the surgery looked to most people like any other month in my life. I kept working every day as a mediator, which meant I was meeting and talking with people all day long. Everyone knew I was going to have the surgery and lots of questions were asked, and I did my best to answer them all. What I really wanted was for the calendar to wind down to let me have my day with the robot and get this tumor out of me.

Finally, Susan and I made the drive back to Louisville to Norton Hospital located in old downtown. It was an unfortunate return to familiar ground for me. I had undergone orthopedic reconstructive surgery there twice when I was a small child. There was no small amount of irony in the moment when I walked through those old Norton doors again some 47 years later to try to save my life on yet another Norton operating table. We checked in and off we went for the 23-hour admission.

I was checked in, gowned up and taken back for the prep for surgery. I honestly don't remember much of it because of the sedation. Susan and my daughter Sarah were there. I had insisted that my son not come because he had important school work that day and I wanted life to go on as normally as possible. Some folks came from the church where I was serving as interim pastor and one of my dearest friends in ministry, Rev. Dr. Mike Lee, drove from Virginia to pray with me and be with Susan and Sarah. The time was at hand. I was wheeled away to the operating room and all went black.

I later learned Dr. Bell came out and gave a great report to all who were in the waiting room. The cancer had not spread and he had taken wide margins of tissue. All looked good.

Was I cured?

No.

Cured is a word you don't get to use in cancer care. Forget about it. Doesn't happen. Cure is the polio vaccine. Cure is the smallpox vaccine. There is no shot a man can take to prevent prostate cancer. There is no cure, only treatment after cancer appears.

What did happen was the routine 23-hour admission. Dr. Bell and another surgeon came by at different times and gave me good reports, but I was so drugged up I could make no sense of them. Susan, who was there, could and she was very pleased and relieved. We were discharged and sent to a nearby hotel to remain in Louisville for one more night in case something happened. I was in good spirits that night owing principally to the large amount of narcotics still in my system. I ordered an extra-large supremo pizza and ate almost all of it by myself. I slept well that night and then it was back in the car for the ride home to London to begin to heal.

***   ***   ***   ***   ***

Healing from surgery is a gradual process. You get to make decisions about how you want to do it. You can beg for all the dope in the world and the health care professionals will, within the limits of their licensure, give you all you want. Or, you can do what I did and refuse pain medication after I left the hospital. I am not a hero. It's just that I was not experiencing enough pain to want pain meds. Now, when I suffered a kidney stone attack a year later, there wasn't enough dope on the planet earth to take away the pain, but that's another story that is minor compared to the cancer journey.

I came home with a catheter in place that allowed the surgical site to heal. The surgeon must sever the bladder from the urethra in order to remove the prostate. For some men, this means they will be incontinent for the rest of their lives. Other men regain their continence within a few hours or days of the surgery. For me, I fell in between the two groups. The catheter was removed 10 days post-op and I went back to work. I wore men's diapers, affectionately called Depends by the company that makes them and by all of us who must use them. I was essentially gravity-driven incontinent for the first month then gradually, week after week, I regained my continence. Now I could walk around in normal underwear instead of the Depends, which had to be changed several times a day.

Post-surgery, the surgeon has several goals. First, he wants to ensure the complete removal of the targeted tissue. Second, restoration of urinary flow with no leakage so there will not be any infection. Third, restoration of continence. Fourth, and perhaps the most important from the cancer perspective, he wants to see the PSA number drop. This will be an indication the cancer is gone. You have to wait for three months to get the first reading.

My PSA was 2.3 when I was diagnosed. This is a really low number for cancer to be present when thinking in the old traditional PSA cancer terms. It used to be no one worried about your PSA unless it was over 4.0. Now, the doctors look at the rate and percentage of movement as indicators of cancer. Mine had gone from 1.3 to 2.3 in one year, which was a significant rise. Now, post-surgery, we would be looking for a drop.

My three-month number brought a smile to Dr. Bell's face. My number had dropped to 0.03. He could not have been more pleased. Anything under 0.1 is considered undetectable, so I was in good shape. Now it could go lower or not. The important thing was for it to stay undetectable over time.

Here is where the waiting thing raises its ugly head again. Cancer patients have to do a lot of waiting. Everything is in the blood for us. Our blood tells us if we are headed in a good or bad direction. It takes time to determine how treatments have worked. You can't hurry treatment.

So began my check-ups every three months, which consisted of PSA blood work and a rectal exam. Why the exam? Well, cancer, if any was left behind, can start growing again and sometimes the surgeon can feel it on the rectal floor. My blood work was always undetectable. So far so good.

Four months post-surgery, I was back on my bicycle riding and doing what I had done before, albeit somewhat more slowly, but at least I was out there. I was working and living and doing the same things I had done before. I did resign from the interim pastor position since the bi-vocational work was too demanding in addition to my regular law practice.

The number was still out there as life went on. The days before an appointment were, and still are, filled with anxiety as I waited on the number and its meaning.

After a year of blood tests, my number moved upward. Still in the undetectable range, but it had moved. It was time for a talk with Dr. Bell. As work matters would have it, I was working in Louisville that day and went to this appointment alone. It was time for me to ask him what he thought. Had the surgery done its job?

His answer was yes, even if there was a remnant of cancer still there. This was so because instead of there being billions of cancer cells present in an engine of an aggressive tumor, there was now only a tiny fraction of that remaining, if at all, and it would take a decade before they would grow sufficiently to cause me trouble.

That was all well and good, but what I wanted to know was whether the cancer was there. I had read that post-cancer surgery

PSA's could produce many false positives because of microscopic remnants of prostate tissue still being attached to the face of the bladder.

Dr. Bell agreed with my laymen's understanding and went on to say there was a one-out-of-three chance some small remnant of cancer remained. He suggested another blood test to see if it ticked up again while I thought things over.

The next blood test did in fact tick up again, but still in the undetectable range. Less than 0.1. As far as a statistician was concerned, I was cured. Now for the odds game. If you are over the age of 70 and get my numbers, then the doctors don't do anything. The math is on your side in terms of outliving the disease if it is present. If you are under 60, which I was, then things become more problematic. If the cancer is there, you need to treat it in order to outlive it. If it is not present, then you are treating your body for nothing.

Dr. Bell wanted me to be on the safe side and undergo combined radiation and hormone ablation therapy to give me the best chance of a cure. There's that word again. Susan and I immediately agreed. The one-out-of-three, while on my side, was still too close to call, too much of a chance to take with my life. He gave me the first hormone ablation shot that hour and then scheduled me for a radiation appointment at the Markey Cancer Center at the University of Kentucky Albert B. Chandler Medical Center.

The shot would prevent my body from making testosterone for six months. I would receive another shot six months later to keep me in testosterone abeyance. In effect, I was entering male menopause with all the hot flashes, mood swings and osteopenia risks a woman has when in menopause. It was no fun, but it was part of the deal. Do it to live.

I was at Markey the next week and was set up for 37 radiation sessions. These took place Monday through Friday of each week until they were completed. I took the first batter up slot at 7:00 a.m. each morning, meaning I had to drive from my home in London to Lexington, a drive of one-and-a-half hours. I would get up each morning at 4:30, go do the treatment and then be at my desk at work by 8:45. It was not bad. You just get in a rhythm and do it. I likened it to training for a marathon, which I have done in the past. You just get in a rhythm and before you know it, the routine becomes commonplace and what others perceive as a burden and a sacrifice is just the life you live. It becomes who you are and you go on with the rest of your life as well.

***   ***   ***   ***   ***

Radiation is not to be undertaken lightly. It is a dangerous procedure that greatly enhances the patient's chances of developing a sarcoma later in life. About a one-in-300 chance. There goes that odds thing again. Still, the radiation guys like their work and report great success with the treatment, and the FDA agrees, so I agreed as well. My radiation oncologists reported very high remission rates with radiation alone therapy and even higher with the combined radiation/hormone ablation therapy. I was off to the races with more treatment.

My mornings in the radiation center were sobering, to say the least. Every time slot has its group of patients. My group was composed of other men who were being treated for serious head and neck cancers. In addition to them, there was one other prostate cancer patient. He and I had it easy compared to the head and neck patients. My treatments lasted about 170 seconds each day. The treatments for the head and neck guys were anywhere from 30 to 40 minutes each day. They were terribly burned and injured by these treatments as they sought to extend their lives. By contrast, my treatments gave me no outwardly discernible side effects. In fact, I became so worried about the lack of side effects that I complained to Dr. St. Clair, my radiation oncologist, who reassured me the radiation was doing its job and that I, in fact, was burned raw inside and would feel the effects and be passing blood by the end of the treatment cycle.

I consider myself one of the blessed after watching my radiation head and neck buddies endure their treatments. Some did not live to finish. Others lived, but suffered greatly. As it was, I completed the 37 treatments with some very mild diarrhea and a tiny amount of bleeding. The week my treatment ended, I went to Hilton Head and walked 36 holes at Harbourtown Golf Course shooting in the 80s. I was pleased.

Subsequent blood tests have been really good. Really low. Whether they stay that way is unknown. My prognosis is good and I

21

am now a permanent patient in the world of cancer care. I work as much as I ever did before and I am as active as I was before. I am here for my family and my work. All of that has been what I hoped would happen, but the reality is it has not been easy by any means. Cancer hurt me and it changed me. Had I allowed it to, cancer could have changed me for the worse.

What I've just shared with you is the technical part of the story. It's the numbers and the tests and the procedures and the side effects. It's the diapers and catheters and radiation machines and odds and statistics. All of that is present in my life, but none of that is me. I am there in the midst of all that stuff. I am not who I was when I entered the world of cancer.

I came to see myself as a caterpillar going into the world of life as a cancer patient. What I became after the surgery and follow-up treatments is where this book really begins. Brian the Caterpillar had been wounded, hurt beyond anything he had ever thought would happen to him. Some caterpillars live long enough to enter a cocoon. Cancer treatment had delivered me to the cocoon stage. Unlike the literal cocoon of the caterpillar, which is a state of inert dormancy while change occurs, my cocoon was dynamic and fluid and shocking to me as I changed in order to survive.

It's time for you to go inside my cocoon.

Welcome to the journey of The Butterfly Man.

Chapter 2

Cocoon

Walking Through the Darkness

There is a darkness that comes with being a cancer patient. We don't talk about it, but it's there. It's unavoidable. The darkness is part of the void created by the cancer sucking the innocence out of the cancer patient's life. Imagine a great, black storm cloud coming over your house and just staying there, never moving. Occasionally it rains and it looks like a final, massive tornado is coming to obliterate your house, but it just hasn't arrived. That's the darkness of cancer.

If you are a fighter like me, then think of the dark of night before battle. You are preparing to stand up and run forward out of the trenches to kill those who would kill you. The outcome of the battle is uncertain as it is in all wars. The only certainty is that you must fight or die. Every warrior must individually prepare themselves for battle. You do the best you can in those dark hours before dawn, and then it's up and over, out of the trenches and into battle. You are on your own Flanders Fields and cancer is your enemy. The fighting is actually easier than the waiting because in battle you are doing something. You have hold of the enemy. You are killing him. Taking his life so that you may live. It is visceral, brutal and necessary.

There are many battles for cancer patients. Many dark nights of searching the soul before going into battle. We face the darkness regularly and still live with the storm cloud over our house. There is sunshine out there, but it can be a long time in coming.

Take the darkness as a given for cancer patients. It's part of our lives. What is more important to the quality of our lives and our survival is how we handle the darkness that surrounds our souls. How we deal with the darkness determines whether we will ever come out of the cocoon.

It is possible to live and function in an entirely normal fashion while living in total darkness. I know because I did it for over a year after I was diagnosed. I lived in the fear of imminent death having experienced the loss of the normalcy of my prior life and still went to work and acted as I always did. I still preached in churches and spoke passionately about the God who loves me and wants us to love each other. I loved my family and did the things that gave back quality of life to them and, on the surface at least, to me. Still, in the back of my mind there was always the fear and dread of dying soon and being powerless to do anything about it. To use a biblical analogy, I was "walking through the valley of the shadow of death." It was not a fun place to be. I basically walked through it in three stages.

    ***   ***   ***   ***   ***

Stage One occurred at the very beginning of my diagnosis and treatment. I focused on understanding what was going on inside my body and what could be done to help me get better. Those were the days of tests, appointments, surgeries and radiation treatments. I focused on the short-term goals of post-operative recovery and returning to prior activities.

Stage Two was my real worry phase, the time when I obsessed over the things I could not control like my bloodwork. I talked too much about it to my wife and friends and I thought constantly about it. I read clandestinely at night about my condition, calculating survival rates and recurrence rates and learned to make the vital and necessary distinction between the two. Finally, with Susan's help I reached the point where I was able to live within the context of "the living game" as opposed to the always unobtainable "going back to the way it was." How I got there has a lot to do with Stage Three.

Stage Three was the most interesting stage of all. I liken it to someone finally deciding to clean out their house after living in it for years. It was a time of looking at my life and getting rid of the clutter and detritus that gradually oozes into life and creates unnecessary distractions and stress. Most of that clutter comes in the form of bad people or at least people who were bad for me. Santa and Jesus may love them and bring them presents, but they did not need to be in my life any longer.

I did not make a conscious decision to fire anyone from my life. It's just that I came to realize I only had so much energy, so much of me to go around and I wasn't going to waste what I had on negative people. Serious illness has a way of drawing into tight focus those people who really matter to you, the ones you really love. These are the indispensables. Everyone else, well they are out there, but they are not part of the circle of survival.

My family, always so very important to me, became even more important. I need to be candid here. I am not talking about blood relatives, which is usually the identifying distinctive for family here in the mountains. By family, I mean those people who drew near to me and hung with me from the beginning. Family, as I painfully learned, can fade quickly away when illness comes. Some of my blood family never darkened my door. They were nowhere to be found. For whatever reason, they could not get down in the trenches with me and fight. The same applied to some of the folks whom I had served faithfully as pastor in prior years. They were absent. Gone. Silent. But here's the good news: Others came to take their place. A phone call here, an unexpected visit from an old football teammate one afternoon, visits from friends who live out of state, cards from churches throughout the county began pouring in. I soon realized I was not alone, that others were remembering me even though some had not. I learned to treasure those who stood with me and to not dwell on those who walked away.

Living as a minister who has cancer is a strange experience. I will simply say my core faith as a follower of Jesus Christ remains. What is gone is my patience and tolerance for the bureaucracy and mind-numbing politics of the church. I was serving a church when I was diagnosed. I concluded that service soon after my surgery because of the distance involved in traveling to that church. It was not long before another church asked me to serve them and I agreed. Over the course of the next year I came to realize I no longer had the patience or calling to deal with the issues that ebb and flow in the life of little churches. My energies were probably never intended to go that far and certainly were not going to be used in that arena following all that I had endured as a cancer patient, so I resigned from that position.

You develop a clarity of perspective when going through

cancer. It is easier to separate the wheat from the chaff. So, after drawing my family close and shedding the aggravation of worrisome churches, I was left with what had always been the core of my life: my family, my faith, my very few precious friends, my profession as a lawyer and my life as a writer. I let everything else go and that is where I remain today.

Now as you might expect, there was some significant overlap between these stages, but what is important is to understand they were the essential, strong undercurrent of my life in that initial new life as a cancer patient. I was in the cocoon and it was a cleaner, healthier place for me to be.

My days at work were fortunately filled with activity. If there is a good part to prostate cancer, it is that you can continue to function normally and for this I am so very thankful. I still have my voice, my mobility and my cognitive functions. I can get on with life.

What was going on inside me, though, was dark indeed. I could convene mediations, talk to the parties and be fully engaged in a substantive dialogue about the pertinent law and facts of the case, and at the same time, in the back of my mind, I would be thinking, "You are not like these people. They are innocent and untouched. They have a real future. You do not."

Gradually, my perspective began to shift. Part of that shift was brought about by people who would confide to me during a mediation or who would call me during the day to tell me they had been treated for prostate cancer or another cancer and they were "still here." I was beginning to understand a lot of people had made this walk and were still here and getting on with life.

This regular encounter with other survivors allowed me to understand and accept my condition. I had not been cursed. God was not punishing me. I simply had an illness. We are all going to die anyway. Some people will die sooner than others, but in the end we all die. What matters is what we do with our lives while we are here.

I would be remiss as a minister if I did not deal with my theology in light of cancer. Let me do that now since it constitutes a substantive part, but not the whole of framing this book. I think by the time you finish reading this book, you will realize I am not your ordinary minister and I thank God for that. I am not hung up on orthodoxy or sanitized language. I lay my life out for all to examine.

I simply love people, all people, because God first loved me and has commanded me to love others. I love straights, gays and people of all races, ethnicities and religious affiliations. I accept as an article of faith that professing Christians go to heaven. I also believe we will run into lots of Muslims, Hindus, Jews and just plain nice people when we get there. I read my Bible, but I'm okay with you reading something else. I practice the compassion of Jesus Christ before anything else.

Cancer did not change any of that. My relationship with God remained rock solid throughout all of this because my theology has never been predicated on God saving my physical body from suffering and destruction. If his Son could endure those things, then why should I be above them? What God promised me through the death of Jesus on the Cross and His resurrection was eternal life for my soul. I believed in that gift and accepted it decades before I had cancer and I believe it now. God is a good God and worthy of praise, even if the cancer comes back.

With my faith secure and the clutter beginning to be removed from my life, I was able to stir in the cocoon a little and start the process of me being me again. And just who was I? I think cancer patients sometimes lose sight of who they are post-treatment. Some people go completely off the rails and leave their old lives behind. Some become spendthrifts and bankrupt their families. Others find a new partner and start new families. Me? I wanted to go back to the me that had been through the first 55 years since it had been a really good 55 years. So who was the old me?

I guess you could say I have always been a busy person. I graduated from college in three years, law school in two-and-a-half and went to seminary at nights while working full-time and raising a young family. I wrote poetry and short stories and a few were published. Add to that scuba diving, hunting Cape buffalo on safari in Africa, caribou in Alaska, bear in Arizona, deer and antelope all over the west and writing magazine articles about those experiences. Add more—staying involved with all of my children's sports and activities, running marathons, bicycling for years, horses, motorcycles, camping, hiking, serving as a bi-vocational minister—all while trying lawsuits for decades and mediating over 15,000 cases, and you could safely say I kept a full plate and I liked it that way. I wanted to return to that life, to wring every last ounce of doing out of my days. What I could not accept at the beginning of my diagnosis and will not accept now is that cancer gives the person who has cancer a license to surrender their life into a recliner and do nothing.

Being in my cocoon became a busy place. It was not solitary by any means and it certainly was not physically or intellectually dormant. To be in a cocoon is to undergo transformation, to be reborn into something different, and that is certainly what was happening to me.

Sometimes transformation involves going back, way back into your past to rediscover things that had been good once before and could be good again. It can mean finding therapeutic benefit in things that had been of benefit before, though others might disagree. It is a singular perspective for the one undergoing transformation. It was finding joy in something that had brought joy before. It was the renewed vigor that came with the setting of a new goal, a new challenge that involved substantial risk and chance. That had been my life before and I wanted it back, but in a different way.

I wrote one book about ministry in the mountains and set it aside. I got back on the road on my bicycle and loved it as much as before. I went back to my cross country hikes off trail in the Daniel Boone National Forest. I started hunting again. It was all good, but I needed more.

I had declared years ago I would see the west on my own, that I would make a solitary journey riding off into the western horizon and let the road take me where it would. I would travel for weeks alone, taking the Great Plains and then the deserts of the Southwest as they came to me with the dawning of each new day. I would meet people and make new friends. I would encounter danger and unknown problems and it would all be good. I would let the trip measure me and make of me whatever it would.

Things began coming back to me. Long forgotten sounds and smells and memories from things I did years ago. The smell of leather in the sun, hot rubber on heat blistered asphalt. The roar and life-pulsing vibration of an engine sitting between my legs. The comforting pressure of body armor, helmets, gloves and boots wrapping me in a literal cocoon for hours each day. The landscape a blur as I leaned over, ever farther, ever closer to the road whizzing by 18 inches under me. This thing must be done right. There is little to no room for error. For the one who does this thing and does it right, it means he is in control and willingly entering into risk and accepting a chance he can discard, but knows he never will.

It meant pulling out old maps and tracing routes with my finger and believing I would live long enough to make the journey.

I did those things and more.

I rediscovered motorcycles.

I did the most dangerous of things and got back on the bike.

I now had a two-wheeled friend in my cocoon.

Chapter 3

Cocoon

Back to the Bike

So, how does a sane, hard-working professional with three college degrees, a wonderful family, a dog, a cat and a better than average golf game get into motorcycles? Basically, all it takes is for your life to get put through the wringer of cancer and then things that seem out of touch, remote and in the past come running back.

I thought motorcycles were a thing of the past for me. Something I did as a boy and young man, but now firmly on the shelf of the things I had done but would never do again. I had always liked them, but there were other things that occupied my time as a young father that made it appropriate to put the bike away. Things like coaching my children's Little League teams, attending dance recitals, teaching Sunday school, maintaining an active trial practice and going to seminary at night after work. My plate was full and I had other things on my mind.

I like riding anything with a saddle on it. I can't begin to count the miles I've ridden on my fleet of bicycles. If I owned a farm, I would have horses to ride like I did when I was a boy. As it is, I go to stables and ride someone else's and am glad to get the opportunity. But motorcycles? Well, that's a different thing altogether as far as non-riders are concerned.

The non-rider looks at a motorcycle and sees certain death or the remainder of someone's life spent in a coma or hooked up to a feeding tube. My friends who are doctors, EMTs and police officers all have stories about the mangled corpses they have seen as a result of working motorcycle accidents. They do their dead level best to scare me and other riders off the bike. Here's why those arguments never work:

For every motorcyclist killed or maimed in a wreck, there are thousands upon thousands of automobile drivers and passengers who are killed or maimed in their cars. It is just which wreck you choose to look at to make your argument. For every vegetative motorcyclist in a nursing home as a result of accident injuries, there are hundreds of thousands of people with dementia sitting in nursing homes having lived careful, safe lives, having never done anything out of fear of what might have happened to them if they had ventured out, taken a chance and journeyed into the unknown. Now they live out their days as carefully maintained wards of for-profit nursing home companies which take the personal assets of the nursing home patient and then proceed to bill the hell out of the government to keep the demented person alive, and to what beneficial personal or societal end?

Sound like how you want your life to end up? I thought so. The difference between a motorcycle rider and those "safe people" is the motorcycle rider has looked beyond the horizon and knows what awaits. It's what you do before you get there, before you get to the Memory Care Unit of Sunnyside Home for the Elderly, that makes life worth living.

When you have cancer, the horizon is closer than it is for others, so the cancer patient takes a hard look at the days remaining before he crosses over to the other side. Some cancer patients take the scared approach and just sit down and wait for the Grim Reaper to come a-knockin'. That wasn't how I was going to go out. I was determined to live every day of my life and live it to its fullest. That meant more hugs, more laughter, reading more, writing more, talking more, working like before, loving more and helping others along the way.

When I was in my late 20s and early 30s, I really wanted to ride a motorcycle across country to the American West. I talked to some of my friends who rode and tried to get them to make the trip with me. None of them wanted to tackle a trip of that magnitude. They were more than willing to take a week off and go with a group of guys to Myrtle Beach to play golf and hit the strip clubs, but a simple ride out west? Not going to happen. So, I gave up, sold my bike and moved onto other things.

As the years went on, I found myself out west over and over again on hunting trips, vacations and attending sporting events. I fell in love with the southwest and the history and places of the Old

West. I traveled there several times with an old law school buddy who shared my love of the lore of the lawmen, gunfighters and gamblers of places like Tombstone, Creed, Lordsburg, Contention and Bisbee. I vacationed with my family at Mesa Verde and Monument Valley. Years later, my son and I took a father-son trip before his wedding to Tombstone so I could share my love of that area's history with him. We had a great time walking the streets where Wyatt Earp and Doc Holliday made history gunning down the bad guys in the Shootout at the OK Corral. We made our way to the old mining town of Bisbee and enjoyed their breweries and mines on beautiful blue sky days when we had all the time in the world to walk and talk and enjoy being alive. Later in the trip, we took a day and rode the ski lift to the top of Mt. Lemon so we could gaze out over the vastness of the valley that is the home for Tucson.

Now here I was, post-surgery and radiation and struggling with the darkness of living with the cloud of cancer. I needed to get away from this small town eastern Kentucky life for a while. I needed to put some distance between the sights and sounds I had come to associate with cancer and cancer treatment. No place heals me quite like the deserts of the southwest. I had to get there and I needed to do it alone. I know the southwest well and I wanted to go there on my motorcycle. It would be my celebration for having endured this thing called cancer. I would be, in a very modern way, a desert mystic making my journey into the arid, lifeless open spaces of the land where nothing lives in order for me to regain some perspective of life and perhaps a renewed energy to get on with living. There was a small problem.

I did not own a motorcycle.

Not owning a motorcycle is a huge problem if your wife is strongly, let's say vociferously opposed to you, the cancer survivor, taking what she sees as an insane motorcycle trip out west. Like the Germans defending Normandy in World War II, wives who "oppose the ride" begin to throw up a formidable array of defenses to prevent the aspiring western rider from ever getting so much as a toehold back on the bike. It begins with what I call the "Constant Harangue." This front line of defense involves said wife informing cancer survivor husband that, "We are not even going to talk about it, it is not a point for discussion in this house, we need to focus on things that make sense and don't you know, the children and I love you and need you!"

There she goes, pulling at the heartstrings to push me away from the bike. This strategy works for a while, but motorcycle shops know this. That is why they keep their inventory shiny and polished and advertise in golf magazines and get Hollywood to make stupid movies that appeal to middle-aged men like *Wild Hogs.* The motorcycle companies then sit back and wait. They are good at this kind of waiting because time, or rather the dwindling amount of time for middle-aged men, is on their side and they know it.

I listened to Susan's arguments and they made sense on that stay-safe-so-the-nursing-home-can-get-all-our-money-at-the-end level. Still, I found opportunities to visit motorcycle stores on days when I was working in Lexington. I began by just walking in and looking around. That was the start of the process of finding a bike. I had no idea what I wanted. My last bike had been a Harley and quite frankly I had not liked it very much at all compared to my old dirt bikes and Enduros. The Harley was cumbersome, top-heavy and hard as hell to steer. It looked great riding down the bypass to get ice cream at our local Dairy Queen, but I knew I would get killed on the thing if I tried to ride it over technical roads. Other riders see it differently, but that was how I saw it from the seat of the bike. But I visited the Harley store anyway. Didn't work for me. I wanted a bike I could ride on dirt roads and over mud, sand and gravel. I wanted to be able to ride standing on the pegs like I had learned when I was a boy. Harley's are just not designed for those things. Motorcycling is very much a to-each-his-own endeavor where the rider chooses the bike based on the purpose. I would ride a lot on pavement, but I wanted the option to go where I wanted when I wanted, and as pretty as the big Harley cruisers were, they would not work for me. The bike was a linkage to going back out on the edge, to being independent and setting my own course as opposed to the rigid course of cancer therapy. The last thing in the world I would ever want would be to buy a bike that would limit my options. Cancer had already done enough of that to me. My problem as a purchaser returning to the motorcycle market arose from having been absent from motorcycling for so many years. I had no idea what was out there and as I found out, my ignorance led to some costly mistakes at the beginning.

I had my moment looking at Harley inventory and then

moved onto other motorcycle stores and, don't you know, there are lots of them, although the inventory has changed. When I was a boy, there were a few models of street bikes and then what we called dirt bikes. You chose between the two and if one did not exactly meet your needs, you bought it anyway and took it home to your garage and modified it to do what you wanted it to do. Fast forward to 2013 and the modern motorcycle store is unrecognizable. Gone is that comforting grease and gasoline smell. Gone is the mechanic/salesman with a grease rag in his hands trying to sell you a bike. He has been replaced by a young guy or girl wearing rapper clothes and baseball caps with the stickers still on. Go to the BMW motorcycle stores and you get guys in polo shirts who offer you freshly brewed coffee and bottled water. It's a different game out there.

I wanted a bike. I didn't know the terminology. I wasn't sure what I could handle. I wanted to have fun. I wanted to live! I wanted a shiny, new bike. I walked into these stores wearing my enthusiasm on my sleeve and pretty much just stood out as a perfect salesman's target. Show me something shiny and new and I was a likely buyer. Just tell me it would work for me (and that I looked good sitting on the thing) and I lapped it up like a kitten at her milk bowl.

One afternoon I visited a local shop. There, sitting on the showroom floor was an old style cruiser completely dressed out with a nice windshield, black Concho-ornamented saddlebags and enough chrome to blind oncoming traffic from a mile away. It could not do any of the things I wanted it to do, but that was beside the point to my out-of-practice riding mind. I had owned one of these before, but not this shiny, not this *cool.* So, I did what a lot of consumers do and I made the impulse buy. I bought a cruiser bike that looked like a Harley, but was made by Kawasaki. This new bike of mine even had whitewall tires. Forget that my feet were positioned so far out in front of me there was no way I could ever stand up on the footboards. Forget that this bike would never go off-road. It was beautiful and shiny and chromed and it was going to be my bike till the day I died decades in the future.

It was a terrible bike.

It rode like a drunken sailor weaving down an alley in the dark. An hour on that thing and my ass was so numb I could have been stung by a nest full of hornets and would never have known it.

It did not block the wind. My head was buffeted so hard by the wind blast that I had a headache every time I rode what soon became to me a green devil monster. I had done what many new buyers do. I had bought with my heart and not my head. I had made one really expensive mistake.

The mistake was compounded by the hell I took at home from Susan for buying the thing in the first place. Her first line of opposition to my motorcycle life had been the unwavering, unremitting vitriol of her attack. I knew there would be no changing her mind with my patient dialogue, so I had employed the time-honored tactic of all great battlefield generals: it's easier to ask for forgiveness than it is to get permission. I bought it without telling her I was going to do so. The bike just sort of showed up at the house when the shop dropped it off in the driveway. This, my friends, is a dangerous strategy because the wife's first line of defense will be replaced, upon finding out the husband has gone ahead and bought the bike anyway, with the frontal attack of giving said husband general, unremitting, 24-hours-a-day hell for weeks on end, it being her goal to badger her husband into taking the thing back. Motorcycle companies know this give-them-hell defense is out there and guess what? They won't take their motorcycles back! You buy one of these babies and it really is yours, and if your wife is going to keep all the lights in the bedroom on every night and scream at you until her lungs come out, well, that's the life of a biker, buddy, and you damn well better get used to it.

I rode the new bike for a few months, enduring the bad ride, the sloppy handling and the constant compromises that come from riding old technology. This bike would be fine for a two-mile ride around town, but it was otherwise a complete and total bust. I needed to move this thing on and find a bike that worked. So, after just two months the search was on and it was going to come at a price because I would have to take a financial hit to get rid of the death trap Kawasaki and come up with a bike that would do what I wanted it to do.

I decided to use the lawyer side of my brain like I should have done at the beginning of my bike quest and be methodical about extricating myself from the abyss of the bad bike. I went ahead and subscribed to numerous motorcycle magazines. I got online and read every blog, website and Facebook page I could find about different kinds of bikes for different purposes. Finally, after weeks of reading I stumbled upon a type of motorcycle called the "adventure bike."

Adventure bike. I liked the sound of that bike. I wanted adventure. I wanted to get out in the world and see things, do things, scream at the top of my lungs, "I'm still here cancer, you bastard! You've not killed me yet!" This was a bike that could go on road or off-road and carry a lot of gear while doing so. It was made with the foot pegs situated underneath and in line with the rider's hips as he sits on the bike, which means the rider can stand up on the pegs and ride. Harley riders can't do that since their foot pegs are so far out in front. They are condemned to sitting all day while riding, which makes any serious off-road riding out of the question.

It turned out there were several companies making adventure bikes and now it was up to me to find one, which I soon did. The problem soon became readily apparent. Men my age were all discovering adventure bikes at the same time which made them much harder to find in stock on a dealer's showroom floor. The Harley guys are still by far and away the most numerous, but the ADV guys, as we are called, are a growing demographic and the number of ADV bikes is barely keeping up with the demand.

By now it was winter 2013. No one wanted a motorcycle now. Bikes had been put up for the winter. It was cold. It had started spitting snow. No dealer would ever take a bike in on trade. If you wanted a bike, it would be better to wait until spring 2014 to make a deal and have a chance of trading your old bike in at that time. I understood all of this. Spring 2014 would be the time to do it, which is why I went ahead and made a deal and bought my new ADV bike in the winter of 2013. You do stuff like that as a cancer patient because there is no guarantee you are going to have a spring like other people.

I was going to take a hit on the trade anyway. I got that. I knew I could not get someone else, much less a motorcycle dealer, to forgive my impulsive first purchase. That was entirely on me and it was solely my choice how long I allowed this mistake to take up space in my garage. Not long, I decided, even if I did lose $3,000 on the deal. I rationalized my mistake by concluding it really was not much of a loss compared to the certain emergency room bills and physical therapy charges that would be headed my way after I crashed the Kawasaki. The way I looked at it, I had just saved my health and maybe my life by trading the bike at a loss. I was a genius!

What followed was that perfect intersection between a machine and the expectations of the person who bought it. I found and purchased a new mid-sized adventure bike called the Suzuki V-Strom 650. As modern bikes go, its engine size was right in the middle at 650cc's. Some Enduro-style motorcycles are sold to be usable on roads at 250cc. Then there are the big boy ADV's in the 1,000 to 1,200cc range. My 650 V-Strom came with hard-sided luggage cases already mounted on the bike so I was good to go on my travel adventure plans. I had tents, sleeping bags and all the other assorted camping gear already so I was pretty much ready to go.

Even though it was winter, I kept riding. I just put on more layers of clothes and off I went, riding backroads in the nearby Daniel Boone National Forest and in the more rural areas near my home. Weeks turned into months of wintertime riding and I found I was becoming more and more comfortable on the bike. It was my plan to continue to practice and then take the Motorcycle Safety Foundation training course in the spring of 2014 so I could obtain my motorcycle operator's license. I was trying to do the thing correctly.

Susan, in the meantime, was persistent in her objection to the motorcycle. She watched me accumulate my gear, the helmet, the armored jackets and pants, the gloves and all the modifications I made to the bike. Periodically, she would turn to me and voice her objections. One day it boiled over with her saying, "Why are you doing this? This isn't like you. You could get hit by a truck!"

My reply was immediate.

"Baby, I've already been hit by a truck. I've had cancer."

And there the line was drawn. Cancer takes away the ordinary perspective of life that non-cancer people are privileged to enjoy. Cancer patients know better than to take out a new mortgage on a house or buy a car using extended payment terms. Life for us is just one whole hell of a lot less certain. Likewise, cancer patients don't have the same fear level as non-cancer folks do. A truck running over me? You want me to be terrified of something I can see? That makes noise? That at least I have a chance of detecting and getting out of the way before it causes me so much as the slightest scratch? Don't think so. Bring it on.

Let me tell you what is truly terrifying. It's waking up one morning feeling perfectly fine and then getting a call while you are at work and being told you have a highly aggressive cancer and that it may be too late to treat you. It's not someone with a gun that I can fight. It's not that infamous truck running over me. It's cancer, and cancer bears some understanding if you are ever going to emerge from the cocoon a better person.

Cancer is not a parasite you swallow that takes up residence in your body. It's not a virus. It's not bacteria. Cancer is worse than all of those. Much worse. Cancer happens when your body, for reasons scientists are working hard to understand, decides to make cells that attack and kill other cells. Cancer cells are the super cells, the musclebound killers that can beat anything in your body. Because your body produces these killer cells, your body doesn't recognize them as a threat. Our bodies' defenses are designed to fight off things that come from the outside like the flu. Those defenses are wonderfully effective against outside elements, but are worthless against cancer. Cancer is the ultimate Trojan Horse or, for those of you who don't read classical literature, the ultimate stealth bomber. Cancer flies under the radar and works its deadly work until it kills the very thing that gives it life—the host body. That's why so much of cancer research today is concentrated on finding a way to make the body recognize cancer as bad and then trigger the body's autoimmune defenses to attack and kill the cancer. This is an emerging area of cancer research and, in my humble opinion, it is where the "cure" will occur. In the meantime, cancer is treated by very old and very conventional means.

In the old days, think Founding Father John Adams' daughter having a mastectomy in the 1700s, cancer was treated by cutting it out or by burning the cancerous tissue with a cauterizing device. They used a red hot poker stoked in an open fire to burn the cancerous lesions away. Surely, you think, here in 2012 we have emerged a more enlightened and more capable people. We must have moved beyond such medical barbarism. My answer is "yes," we are an evolved people when it comes to having sources of irrelevant entertainment like iPads and XBoxes. Not so much when it comes to treating cancer.

My cancer was treated by first cutting it out and then, for

round two of my therapy, setting it on fire. The cutting was done using a DaVinci robot, but it was a knife just like in the 1700s. My surgeon simply looked at the cancer and started slicing parts of my body out and throwing them in the garbage can. The burning was done by radiation, but my insides were burned until I leaked blood. Primitive work by any standard. We can do better and that is why research, including stem cell research, must continue with full government funding and support. My hope is that the cutting and burning got rid of my cancer, but in truth I would feel a whole lot better if something more modern had been available for me.

This kind of treatment, even though it is most often effective, leaves lingering doubts in the mind of the cancer patient.

"What if they missed a cell? What if the radiation machine missed the target? What if the surgeon missed the margins? What if…" It just goes on and on and if the target was missed, then those super cells, those always deadly cancer cells will come back to attack me again and this time they will be like Alexander's army: they will be on the move with a rapid vengeance.

So, show your ignorance and tell me I can get killed by a truck.

Marvelous! It means no Hospice. No weighing 70 pounds at the end and looking like I have been in a prison camp. No intractable pain that not even heroin can dent. Dying on my bike means that I can, by God, go out in full vigor on my terms, dying in God's glorious open air and not in some sterile room surrounded by people wearing blue gloves and pumping me full of worthless medicines that can't stop the cancer.

Getting killed by a truck?

I'll take it. Order me one up right now. Just don't expect me to willingly ride straight into the truck's path. I look forward to fighting to avoid the bastard and making a good game of it.

I more or less explained my thinking to Susan, and while she did not agree, she did at least listen. I continued to ride the bike during the winter of 2013-2014. I rode to understand the sport of the bike better. More importantly, I rode to live. I was doing something different, exploring a new horizon, preparing to go where I had not really gone before. If cancer is the great denier of dreams, then I was determined to deny cancer a few of its own and get out ahead of it and do my thing. The bike was simply an expression of my resistance to the disease.

I became a solitary rider. There are plenty of guys who live near me who are riders and they invited me to ride with them, but I declined. Just as cancer is a solitary journey, so it evolved that I became a solitary rider. My afternoon and weekend rides would wind through Laurel County down to Lake Cumberland and Laurel Lake, at times over to the Cumberland Gap in Middlesboro and up into the Bluegrass around Berea and Danville. I was exploring and learning about myself and the bike at the same time.

I had worried about my ability to maneuver something as heavy as a motorcycle, but I found I could do it just as I had done years before. The weight of 500-plus pounds was not insignificant, but the throttle and some thinking ahead made riding it very manageable. The art of riding, clutching, shifting, braking, leaning and placement of the bike in turns requires a great deal of concentration. This mental effort was good for me since it took my mind off of the things I could not control like the return or cure of the cancer. Cancer was the farthest thing from my mind when I was leaning into a curve on a mountain road with no guard rail while facing oncoming traffic, and in that sense my time on the bike has been extremely therapeutic.

By the spring of 2014, I was ready to take my training course and get my license. I set aside a weekend for it and went to Eastern Kentucky University and spent two-and-a-half days there obtaining excellent training and earning my license. I learned a lot about motorcycle safety to be sure, but I also learned I was still capable of doing new things, of stepping outside my comfort zone and embracing physical challenges with the same enthusiasm I had before cancer came along.

In a few weeks, I received a notice in the mail I could go to the Circuit Clerk's office and get my license. I walked up to the office during a lunch break and got the license. I had done it! I had bought a bike, learned how to ride it and had demonstrated my riding ability to the satisfaction of the state. I could now ride my V-Strom wherever and whenever I wanted. I was not only a cancer warrior. I was a kick-ass biker cancer warrior. I liked the sound of that.

It was now spring 2014.

It was time to hit the road and ride.

Chapter 4

Broken Dreams

Tennis Can Screw Up Anything

I had my license, I had my V-Strom adventure motorcycle and I had a plan. I was going to ride on weekends during the summer of 2014 and ride out west during the late fall. I had not zeroed in on a specific destination, but I was going to figure it out while I rode shorter weekend excursions around Kentucky and took advantage of our great state parks and the convenient camping they afford riders like me. These shorter incremental trips would be my period of apprenticeship in preparation for the big ride which I had labeled the "I'm Still Here Ride 2014."

I started by sorting out my camping gear and figuring out just how much I could pack in the side cases and how much I could pack in the waterproof duffle bag I would strap over the back seat. It is a reality of motorcycle touring that there is only so much space for storage on the bike. It became an exercise in mathematics and a sort of philosophy of limited luggage space versus the philosophy of desire. I knew I would have to decide between what I could pack and not overdo it and what I really wanted to take so I could live with all the creature comforts of home like a really, really thick mattress and a fan to stay cool. Those things did not make the final cut of my equipment list, but they were in the mix for far too long.

I began to gather everything up and place it in the center of my basement floor. The process went on for weeks until I looked at the pile and realized I would need a trailer to haul all of the stuff I had assembled. It was obvious I had to get rid of the luxury, keep the necessity and then whittle that down incrementally. Each night after work, I would come home and descend the steps to my basement and get on my bicycle on the trainer for a workout. I kept my gear pile in front of the bike. I would stare at the ever-dwindling pile as I rode and ask myself over and over again as I took mental inventory of my pile, "Do I really need that?" I would finish my hour ride, get off and walk over to the pile, bend down and move another piece or two out and then weigh my decision overnight. Gradually, I began to have a gear pile I could fit onto the motorcycle and still have a stable ride.

Finally, I had the gear issues resolved. My gear was very basic: lightweight one-person tent, ultralight sleeping bag, backpacker sleeping pad, one-person mess kit, stove, fuel, toiletries, basic motorcycle tool kit, clothing and a few odds and ends. Even with that small list, it took up plenty of space on the bike and of course made it heavier, which meant the bike handled differently and required more practice riding with it loaded down with gear.

The bike was in great shape for the trip and I had my gear figured out and packed to ride. While no motorcycle is ever deemed perfect and no gear list is ever 100 percent satisfactory, I was confident I had my gear ready to make a successful trip. My ride to the Columbus-Belmont would cover 340 miles one way and take about six hours. Under normal circumstances, that would be a short day's ride. The problem was me. I was leaving for my Mississippi River trip with a barely healed broken arm and leg, gimping about on a damaged lateral collateral ligament in my left knee and getting over a slight concussion.

What happened, you say? Crash like your wife predicted you would? Make fortune tellers out of your EMT and police buddies who warned you of the dreaded dangers of the demon bike?

Well, no. I owed my injuries, serious as they were, to a sport far more dangerous than riding a motorcycle: I had decided to play tennis.

One of my brother-in-laws is a tennis player. He loves the damn sport. (You are allowed to curse a sport that breaks your bones.) As I was healing from my cancer surgery, he badgered me (you are allowed to say badger when the sport results in broken bones) to buy a racket and take up tennis so we could play together during his retirement. I thought about it and finally, during the summer of 2014 while my son was home on a break from his MBA studies, decided to order a racket and some balls and play tennis with my soon-to-be MBA offspring.

I researched rackets and bought one that seemed appropriate for a middle-aged player. I bought balls, lots of balls. I would need lots of balls because I was going to hit them so hard and knock the hell out of them so much that they would run from me to get off the court and new ones would be sacrificed to my lethal game. While we waited for the racket and case of balls to arrive, my son and I continued to play golf and basketball together. Elliott is an excellent golfer and the two of us have spent countless days walking round after round. It is a sport we both love and know well. Golf is a sport you can play well into old age. I should have stayed with golf.

One afternoon we were in the driveway shooting basketball and having a good time. I was losing, as usual, to my fitter than a Marine son when the UPS truck pulled up. He was delivering my racket and balls.

Oh the joy! The ecstasy! I had a new toy! I had a playmate, my son, whom I could take to the tennis court and wear him out like he was wearing me out on the basketball court. (Confession here, I played a lot of tennis in my younger years and wasn't half bad.) There was no time like the present. The racket and balls were here, the sun was shining and we were burning daylight. It was time to go.

So sure was I of my moment of victory that I invited my wife along to watch me thrash my son about the asphalt courts of the local high school. Victory loves an audience. This was going to be the beginning of my summer of tennis dominance. I was back.

An hour later, I was in the emergency room.

It happened like this, or at least I think it happened like this: My son and I had been playing for about 30 minutes. We were having a good time volleying back and forth. I was out of practice, but I knew what I should be doing even when I did not quite get it done. We decided to play a game. I was wearing my high-topped clunker basketball shoes. I had ordered tennis shoes, but the traitorous tennis shoe company had not delivered them yet. My son hit a volley to my backhand side. It was several feet to my left, but I could reach it. Yes, I could. I had done it a thousand times before a lifetime ago. Surely I could still get over there to that ball before it passed me. All I had to do was run like a fleeing gazelle and stretch out flat. I could get it. I was there! I was getting it! I was down.

Fade to black…

Susan and Elliott said it looked like one long continuous fall as I tripped and tripped again and then hit on my knee, bounced and skidded into the steel fence pole, hitting it with my arm and head. I have no idea what happened. I have not a clue. I was knocked out or stunned for a moment. The next thing I knew Elliott was standing over me. I was in the same position as a worn out boxer on a bad night at Caesar's Palace. I had nowhere to go but up.

"Dad? Dad? You ok? You look hurt."

Pride causes all sorts of problems for people. The refusal to acknowledge and admit you have really screwed things up always leads to an even bigger screw-up. It makes you keep driving without stopping and asking for directions long after you are hopelessly lost. It makes you keep working on the leak under the sink with water spraying everywhere and the plumber just a phone call away. It makes you get back up from the tennis court and keep playing tennis with a broken arm and leg and a concussion.

"I'm fine." I said as I stood up, blood pouring down my arm and knee from the abrasions I sustained in the fall. My arm was completely numb as was my knee. My head felt thick and groggy. "Let's play."

And so we played on. For about 15 minutes we played on until my left arm quit working. I could no longer grip the ball and I could not raise my arm for a ball toss. The leg was holding together, but I was hurt for sure. It was time for pride to take a trip to the Emergency Room.

"Let's go to the hospital. I think I'm hurt."

ER doctors and nurses see it all. In our little corner of the world in southeastern Kentucky, a lot of what they see is drug addicts cruising the ERs for pain pills. These people aren't hurt. They are just hooked on dope and will do anything to get their fix. They rob, steal, murder and lie to get what they need. They are frequent visitors to the ERs of the mountains. Ordinary citizens who are not hooked on dope do not want to be confused with these people. I knew I was hurt as I walked into the ER, but my biggest concern was not to be mistaken for a druggie. In reality, I had no worries in that regard. The blood was by now looking generously good on my arm and leg and I had a really nice bruise on my shoulder. I was beat all to hell. I was not a druggie.

We sat in the waiting room of the ER for about 30 minutes, during which time I watched two obviously high on dope people hallucinate their way around the room. One lady stopped repeatedly to have a conversation with the soft drink machine. From what I could tell, the machine was talking back to the druggie, but the druggie was holding her own in the argument and giving the machine pure hell. Another druggie was trying the nice guy con on the admitting clerk, but you could tell she had seen and heard it all before. She just told him to wait his turn and to go sit down, which he proceeded to do while he executed the addict's scratch to placate the incessant itch addicts have when they need a fix. Just watching him scratch his body made me itch all over. Finally, an aide came out and took me to the triage room for my work-up. I think the blood and torn clothing helped convince him I was a real patient, and from what I saw in the waiting room, I was the only legitimate patient in the ER. I was wheeled into an examining room and in a few minutes x-rayed and given a thorough going over by the emergency room physician, an older gentleman who was amused at the thought of me playing tennis against my much younger son.

A nice nurse came into my room after an hour or so and told me to come out to the x-ray viewing box so she could show me my x-ray. One of the nice things about being a pastor in a small town means the folks who work in the ER get to know you, and one of the privileges, if you can call it that, is you can look at x-ray of your broken arm without having the doctor explain it to you.

My arm was broken so bad even I could see the break. Fortunately, the fracture was still in place, no bones moved or shattered. Just a nice, neat break. The ER having diagnosed me and me having refused painkillers, I was discharged from the hospital and sent home with an appointment to see an orthopedist in Lexington the next week. In the meantime, I was wearing a sling to hold my broken arm in place. I asked to be referred to a group I knew to be very modern in their approach to orthopedics. I also knew one of them rode a V-Strom.

They were more modern than I thought. Dr. Favetto, my V-Strom riding ortho, took one look at the x-ray and agreed I had a dandy of a fracture. I was ready for the cast. I was already thinking of the colors of Sharpies I would carry with me for people to autograph my plaster of Paris attire as their wounded warrior.

"No cast," said my V-Strom riding ortho.

"What do you mean no cast? I have a broken arm, don't I?"

"Yes you do, and if you want it to heal as fast as possible then wear the sling for a week and then start using the arm."

"What is this madness?" I thought to myself. "Surely I need a cast to protect my arm."

"OK. I'll just use the sling."

I left my V-Strom ortho wondering what kind of treatment this was. Just look at my arm and tell me it's broken? I could do that for people! What was the medical degree for if all my doctor did was send me home to lie around like one of my hunting dogs after it has been banged up fighting a raccoon? Still, I really liked the idea of not having to drag a cast around for six weeks. I would show them. I would go out and use the arm and heal in four weeks.

Well, it does not work like that. Bones, it seems, kind of know how long it takes them to heal and six weeks is what it takes for healthy people—read non-smokers here—to heal. As the weeks passed, my arm began to hurt less and my range of motion improved. Strength was secondary, but I was at least moving the arm. After two weeks my arm was doing a lot better, but my left leg was now giving me serious problems.

Notice I have not mentioned my leg to this point. That's because my leg was not on the radar at the ER since I walked into St. Joseph London and walked out on my own. I drove myself to work the following Monday after my fall and walked around the office all day mediating. I had decided that even with a broken arm I could get back on my bicycle and ride on the trainer to keep my legs strong so I finagled around and got myself on the bike and rode with one arm for my usual one-hour training ride. I tried riding with my arm in the sling, but it was just too uncomfortable so I took it off and let my left arm hang to my side and on I rode. My leg seemed fine on the bike, but off the bike it just wasn't working correctly. My gait had changed and I was limping and dragging the leg as I walked. Back I went to my modern orthos.

It turned out my V-Strom ortho only did arms and hands, but he had a non-motorcycle riding partner who took care of legs. In a few hours, I was scanned and back in my new leg ortho's office. He was a grandfatherly type, but just as modern in his approach to fracture care as V-Strom ortho.

"You have a non-displaced fracture of the tibial plateau and either a severely stretched or torn lateral collateral ligament. I'm leaning toward a severe stretch."

"So what do I do?"

"Nothing. It will heal on its own. Keep riding your bike and walking and it will heal over time. It may take two years for the ligament to return to normal."

"I've got a long distance motorcycle trip planned for this fall. Will I be able to ride?" (It was now August.)

"Sure. You'll be fine."

I left the modern ortho office elated that I had once again escaped a cast and surgery. It was good to know I would just heal on my own without any medical intervention of any kind. These are the kinds of things you find out when you go to a modern orthopedic office and pay them over $2,000 to just talk to you. Kind of like how it is when people come to me and receive legal advice. Who am I to complain? Knowledge is the true currency of the world. Anybody can be a mechanic of a surgeon and dig around with scalpels and grinders, but it takes a real physician to look at you and tell you your body can do the job on its own.

I went home and continued to train on the bike and lift weights with my good arm. Finally, after six weeks I was released to all activities. I waited a few more weeks and then got back on my motorcycle. I could pull the clutch with my left hand and shift gears with my left foot. So far so good. The test would be my Mississippi River ride.

***　　***　　***　　***　　***

I left for Columbus-Belmont State Park and the Mississippi River about two months after I had broken my arm and leg. My arm did great, but my knee really hurt after riding for a while. I would ride for about 30 minutes before the leg would start aching and cramping. I soon realized there was no way I was going to make it to the park if I took a break every 30 minutes. So, I rode on with an aching leg and tried to flex the cramps out of it as I rode. That proved to be a very bad idea as the flexing caused my weight to shift on the bike and ended up making the bike wobble badly twice before I gave up on the stretching while driving routine. I was able to keep going for an hour before pulling over to stop and stretch the leg and then get back on and repeat the entire process. This went on for almost eight hours, but I finally made it to the state park campground with daylight to spare.

I had successfully made the 340-mile ride to Columbus-Belmont over uneventful parkways and excellent U.S. highways. The roads were relatively straight with no serious curves or demanding terrain, but, easy as they were, they had taken their toll on my arm and leg. I knew by the time I got there that my ride out west would not be taking place in 2014. I was just too banged up to undertake such a long ride.

It was a disappointing moment to realize my big ride would have to wait, but hurt is hurt and it just takes time to heal. I enjoyed my one-night stay at the campground overlooking the Mississippi and then it was up early the next morning to limp on back home on the bike.

I continued to ride throughout the fall of 2014 and did another overnight trip, but my mind was always on the grand ride I did not take, the one that ended out there on the tennis court. Did I mention I have a tennis racket for sale really cheap?

***　　***　　***　　***　　***

If I have learned anything from my years of participating in sports and pursuing various hobbies like golf, cycling and hunting, it is that the aspirant's acquisition and use of equipment to pursue said hobby or sport is always evolving and usually at a more expensive price point. I have been an avid golfer since I was nine years old and I have a roomful of clubs to prove it. I have been a cyclist equally as long and I have spent as much on my touring bicycles as some people spend on cars. I have convinced myself that all of them are necessary on one level or another, but if I had less money and less options I could make do with just a few of the bicycles and likely have played golf with the same score with the same set of clubs I used back in the 1980s. As I have learned, the same principals apply to the sport of motorcycling.

My first bike was a death trap for me, but someone else might ride it all over the world with no problem. Then came the V-Strom. It is a perfectly acceptable bike. It does all things adequately and will get you there and back. It is affordable as those things go and it is, above all, reliable. In short, it is like that plain girl in high school who was just dying to go to the prom with you, would marry you, make you a good wife, always take care of your house, your kids, your dog and have a hot meal on the table for you every night at six. Except, except, she didn't thrill your heart. As wonderful as she was, she could not make you long for her. She was and would always be fine and good and all the things that make life safe. But she would never set your heart on fire. That was the V-Strom.

It was not that I fell out of love with the V-Strom. My confession is I was never in love with the bike and to throw your leg over a bike and ask it to take you across a continent, you have to love the bike and love the V-Strom I did not. Like former president Jimmy Carter, I had been committing adultery in my heart. I was lusting after another and I could not make it stop. I was in love with the BMW GS.

To the non-biker, you are now understandably lost in the nomenclature of motorcycles. GS is short slang for the BMW R1200 GS motorcycle, an adventure bike that is the pinnacle of all adventure bikes. It is the bike that carried the famous (in travel circles anyway) adventurers and actors Charley Boorman and Ewan McGregor, first all the way around the world from London, England east through Europe, Russia and Mongolia, to Alaska, Canada and the United States, and then on a second trip down the world from Scotland to the tip of South Africa. Their documentary films *Long Way Round* and *Long Way Down* were huge hits in the United Kingdom and here on public television and cable channels. Thousands of DVDs of those adventures have been sold to aspiring travel riders like me and they serve as templates for our efforts to ride ever farther on our motorcycles. Their motorcycles were the BMW GS and, as you might suspect, the bike has become as famous as the men who rode them. Owing principally to being ridden in those films, the GS is now BMW's number one selling motorcycle, delivering millions of dollars a year in revenue to the Bavarian Motor Works.

The GS, as it is affectionately called, is not your father's motorcycle. This bike is a go anywhere, do anything machine. It can cruise comfortably on interstates at 90 mph or it can crawl through bogs and mud where no road exists, and it can do both while carrying the rider and loads of gear. It is a motorcycle for people who want to travel far and wide and get dirty doing it. It has an electronics array to dazzle a jet pilot. It has a shaft final drive, meaning no chain to oil, just a shaft like a car. It is powerful and can go anywhere and do anything the rider has the skill to get it to do. It is a brute and a ballet dancer at the same time. Nothing out there even comes close.

My multiple fractures summer had given me the unexpected gift of more time to refine my riding skills and to make the commitment to sell the always fine and good and reliable V-Strom and buy a GS. I sold the V-Strom in November 2014 and continued my quest for a GS.

While a large part of my GS search took place online, the reality of buying a brand new motorcycle will eventually land the buyer at a dealer. Not all dealers are created equal. I contacted a few BMW dealers since I was going to have to travel to buy a BMW, there being no BMW dealers in my little town.

I had the good fortune at this point to find Chris Horrar, a sales professional at the Louisville BMW dealership. He has a passion for motorcycles for sure, but what made him special for me was his genuine interest in me as a rider and the purpose I was trying to achieve by purchasing a new bike. We talked and emailed for several weeks. He discouraged me from buying faster, sportier models and guided me away from bigger heavier bikes. He suggested the GS as a bike I could handle and handle well. He let me make the decision as any good sales professional would, but his advice was perfect for who I was as a rider given my age and ability level and the touring I wanted to do.

November 29, 2014 was the day I pulled the trigger and bought the GS. This bike was going to go into battle with me and fight this damned cancer. It was going to carry me through rain and wind and desert heat and would never fail me and, in fact, it never did.

You may be looking at the bike and thinking that a Harley is far more beautiful and I suppose you are right from a 1950s aesthetic point of view. But a warhorse is not a show pony. Its purpose is to carry its rider faithfully through the most difficult of circumstances and to always be ready to go. My warhorse of a motorcycle was built for just that kind of work. My GS and I would go into battle together and find our way out of this darkness of cancer that had enveloped my life.

***   ***   ***   ***   ***

Six months later the GS would be clad in armor as would his rider and off to battle we would go.

A lot happened between the day I bought the GS and the day I left on the ride. My normal life of work and family was always there, but "The Journey" was always on my mind. It is one thing to have the desire to undertake a cross continent ride. It is another thing altogether to put a solo ride together, to figure out the dates and route and plan for the contingencies that are part of long distance travel. Some riders plan their route to visit National Parks or battlefields or breweries. Some just ride to a family destination.

Me? I owe my route selection to the United States Air Force.

Chapter 5

The Route

Many Roads, One Destination

No sooner had I bought the GS than the United States Air Force threw me a curve. Actually they threw the curve at my son, but it was in my strike zone as well. The way it all worked out just goes to show you can plan for your kids and think you know how they are going to turn out, and then along comes that thing called independent thinking and out the window goes all your carefully made assumptions about what the future holds for your children.

I have two children. My daughter Sarah is the oldest. She is happily employed in a corporate job in the Bluegrass. My son Elliott was still in college when I was diagnosed with cancer. He graduated with honors in biology and then pursued an MBA at the Gatton School of Business at the University of Kentucky, which was fine by me since I come from a business family.

I was deep in the throes of planning my "I'm Still Here Tour" when Elliott graduated from the Gatton School in 2014. He was ready to apply to dental school or to enter the private sector. I was lobbying for private sector since I had a hard time imagining my college golfer son spending the rest of his life indoors with his hands crammed in the mouth of someone with bad breath. Elliott started interviewing and was living at home with us during the process. He was also engaged to be married to his high school sweetheart as soon as he found real employment. This is all very good. We were excited for Elliott amid the boundless horizon a good education affords. I could see Elliott and me starting a business or at the least playing a lot of golf together after he got his job secured.

One afternoon in late spring, I came home from the office to be greeted with the news the United States Air Force had contacted my son to recruit him to serve in their Medical Service Corps as an officer. I had received similar recruitment contacts from the military when I graduated from law school so I was not surprised. I was rolling with the thing until Elliott told me he had researched the Medical Service Corps and was going to enter into the competitive recruitment process.

Wonderful. I had spent a huge chunk of my life raising my son only to see him join the military and disappear into that blind abyss of moving from one base to another for decades before a well-earned and just as well-funded military pension. He would play lots of golf and get a great tan. I, on the other hand, who wanted nothing more out of life than to spend my elder years playing 18 holes with my businessman son, would be reduced to mere Pabulum-infused rubble at a nursing home unable to do anything and having missed out on years with my son while he traipsed all over the world wearing that beautiful blue uniform of the Air Force.

Still, a good father doesn't stand in the way of his son's dreams, so I did what I always do and I became the enthusiastic cheerleader and facilitator to help my boy get to where he wanted to be.

Elliott was notified in September 2014 he had been accepted into the Medical Service Corps and he could expect to be called to Commissioned Officers Training in the summer of 2015. That was workable with the trip. I could make that work if the kids would just tell me when they wanted to get married.

The children had asked me to perform their wedding. There is no greater privilege for a minister than to perform the wedding of your children, so all we had to do was select a motorcycle-sensitive date and all of us would be happy. I did not voice this, you understand. Doing so would have placed me in the wedding doghouse for probably 20 years or more. I just had to play it out and see how things landed.

The kids selected an April date. Perfect. We could get them married and Elliott could go off to training and be at his base by June. The Air Force assigned him to Holloman Air Force Base near Alamogordo, New Mexico. Life was just getting better and better. Now I was not only making a ride out west, but I had a real reason to make the trip. As any concerned and loving father would do, I had to get myself out to his new town, scope it out, make sure it was safe for my boy and his bride and get a good visit with them at the same time. This logic would, of course, work only with base assignments in the States. Anything outside and I would have to work a bit harder to sell the concept.

I got out my maps and realized I needed more maps. I ordered gobs of maps from the American Automobile Association (AAA). I went to bookstores and bought more. I bought a laminated map of the United States so I could trace routes on it with a grease pen and erase as needed. I bought travel books galore for every state I might conceivably cross during my journey. I loaded maps onto my iPad. Armed with all of this, I began my study of routes across the big Midwest of the Lower 48. I studied temperatures, annual rainfalls, projected construction zones and wind flows. I was working so hard I could have been a battle planner for the Normandy invasion. It is not an understatement to say I was spending most of my free time zoning in on my maps trying to find a route.

Route selection is not easy. If you have a starting point and a destination you at least have two pins to stick on your map. After that, where you go and how you pack for the trip depends on what you want to do and see while you are riding to your destination. Early on I learned that computer program route planners like MapQuest were of only rudimentary help to me as a motorcyclist. I wanted to travel and see the country, not the droning gray and black concrete slabs and asphalt ribbons of the interstate highway system. MapQuest and most of the other planning engines put you on the interstates and leave you there. It is America's most efficient way to travel, but also the most boring. You see very little of the heartland of America, but you make great time. I soon realized time was a precious commodity, but not the only one I would have on the trip. I wanted to balance my time constraints with my desire to pass through little towns and ride the backroads while eating at little cafes and camping when the day ended. I would have to plan my route to maximize my time to meet my objectives.

The nights of map study convinced me I did not want to linger for any extended length of time while crossing the Midwest. I could cover it on shorter trips from my home in Kentucky. I wanted to get on out west on this trip and ride through New Mexico, Arizona and Utah and see the red rock country. I planned to spend the bulk of my time in the west and explore where Elliott and Sydney would be living. All the while, I would be on my bike. I would ride where I pleased, sleep where I wanted and have a schedule of my own making.

Getting through Kentucky would all be on familiar road. After that, I would be covering new ground with every roll of my wheels. Should I go through Missouri? Maybe dropping down through Tennessee to Memphis and then over would be better. I could go through northern Texas or maybe take an extreme southern route through Tennessee and pick up the Natchez Trace and ride across Louisiana into Texas. I could ride through the Big Bend National Park in Texas on my way to Alamogordo. Maybe I could ride through southern Kansas and across Texas and Oklahoma into New Mexico and see Taos and its environs before riding into southern New Mexico and exploring Alamogordo.

Mileage from my home to Alamogordo was approximately 1,500 to 1,750 miles depending on the route I took. That may not sound like a lot, but then think about how many hours a rider has to sit on a bike riding and it becomes an exponentially more challenging task. Drive a car across the country and a 1,500-mile drive can be done in a really long day. You can eat while you drive, reach back into your cooler and get something to drink, change your ambient temperature and adjust the firmness of your seating. Not so for the motorcyclist.

A motorcyclist does well to average 55 mph on a long distance trip even if he is riding at a steady speed of 75 mph. It works like this:

When you are in a car you have very little downtime on the interstate. Most of a car trip is spent in motion. It's a little more complicated on a bike. We touring motorcyclists have to account for every minute of our time in order to correctly estimate travel and, this is very important, arrival times. I found my actual average mph on the trip came to 47.5 mph. Based upon what I read in planning for the trip, I planned on averaging 45 mph so I did not miss the mark by a very wide margin. That meant when I looked at a thousand-mile route I would divide it by 45 and arrive at the number of hours of total travel time required to cover that segment. In the end, I planned on covering about 450 miles a day on the way out. This would be a very doable distance since a lot of riders will ride over 500 miles a day.

I started making tentative route marks with my grease pen on my big map I had tacked to the wall of my corner of the basement I dubbed the "War Room." It became the place where I stored all my gear and began the long process of gearing up from the trip.

My route markings on the big map were to change over and over in the months before the trip.

I decided I would make my trip during the month of June. By then Elliott would be finished with his training and there was a good chance he would be on active duty at Holloman by the time I rode gloriously into Alamogordo. I selected June 3-20 as my trip dates and continued to work on the map. June would be a great month for travel across the Midwest. Fairly mild temperatures, fewer storms and the wedding would long be over so all the tension surrounding the wedding would have long since dissipated.

Then it happened.

Who knew the Air Force could change its mind? Who ever heard of the Air Force amending an officer's dates for training camp? Well, it turns out the military changes its mind all the time and if you don't like it, well, then just get to the back of the line and wait your turn one more time. You are owned by Uncle Sam now, and Uncle Sam does as Uncle Sam damn well pleases.

The Air Force out of the blue (yes, it is a pun) notified Elliott in mid-November 2014 his training date would be moved up to late January 2015. He would be going in with the first training class instead of a later class. I'm sure whoever the genius in Washington was who amended the orders knew just what he or she was doing for the good of the country; however, two families in little London, Kentucky would have been better served if they had been consulted. As it was, the wedding which was planned for April 2015, some five months away, had just been moved up to January 10, 2015, some eight weeks away. Now all the planning that was going to take place in five harried, stress-filled months for the women of the family would now be mercilessly crammed into a six-week temple-bursting pressure capsule of misery that would drive most of us almost insane.

Notice I said "most of us." As the presiding minister, I knew my job well and since I was the only minister in the wedding, no one really got to tell me what to do. Since I am a Christian minister, there are faith constraints on what I can and cannot do in a wedding, not to mention the constraints I place on myself. Most ministers have things they will not permit in their wedding ceremonies and I am no different. Fortunately, my children knew better than to ask me to perform some non-Christian chant or incantation. Have me perform a Christian wedding and that is what you get. Since I knew my job, I could more or less relax. I did write the occasional check or two, but that job falls to the father of the bride and it was not yet my turn for my neck to pass under that particular guillotine so I could rest easy. I would just marry the kids sooner and keep planning my trip.

The women of the family kept it cool for the most part. There was a lot of scurrying around and planning for showers, rehearsal dinner and the wedding proper, but all I had to do was nod and the juggernaut that is the relentless wedding machine just carried on. Elliott and Sydney started packing for the big move to Alamogordo which would take place in the spring. From time to time, I would look in on the packing operation just to make sure they did not pack any of my gear in the countless number of boxes the kids were packing in my basement just a few feet away from the War Room corner.

***   ***   ***   ***   ***

The wedding day came and it was beautiful. I wondered how I would handle performing the actual ceremony since Elliott is my only son. Except for a tiny hitch or two in my throat, I did well. It meant a lot to me to have survived cancer to be able to perform the wedding. It was another one of the very tangible ways I could look at cancer and say, "You didn't take that away from me, you bastard."

I know it is odd to read some of the profanity in this book and reconcile it with knowing the author is a minister. What you have to understand is that bad language is used all the time on a battlefield by the most moral and devout of people, and there is no deadlier or more earnest battlefield than the fight against cancer. It is a life and death struggle every bit as real and serious as any conventional battlefield. I am now a veteran warrior of the first order and not of my choosing, even though I don't have the uniform or medals that military warriors possess. I have been in battle and I am terribly scarred, but I am still here. I lived to perform my son's wedding and kiss the bride. That is one of my many life medals I have earned as a cancer fighter. The profanity is just a warrior's way of screaming away the fear while facing a relentless enemy.

*** *** *** *** ***

Elliott and Sydney went off for their honeymoon after a really nice wedding reception that saw dancing, laughter, cake and more than a few glasses of champagne. Hard to believe he would be going off to camp in 12 days, but orders were orders as we were learning in our family.

  Elliott and Sydney drove to Panama City Beach for a honeymoon at my brother's condominium—a wedding present from Uncle Ernie. They were going to have a long week there before Elliott drove to Maxwell Air Force Base in Montgomery, Alabama to begin his training. The children called us when they got there and then periodically texted us photos of their beach walks and dinners out they were enjoying as a newly married couple. Things had worked out really well. The moms survived a very compressed planning time frame and the dads avoided any serious collateral damage that comes from being essentially worthless when planning a wedding. In my mind, I saw the newlyweds coming back home the following week and then saying goodbye to Elliott as he made the trip south to begin his career as an officer.

*** *** *** *** ***

Did you know the Air Force can re-change its mind? Did you know they can amend orders that have been amended? Yes, they sure can and you can't do a damn thing about it except say, "Yes Sir."

  The Air Force texted Elliott midway through his honeymoon and let him know his training camp date was being pushed back to August 2015, some eight months away. There was no appeal, no recourse. Orders are just orders and that is the way it is my friends.

  Let me get this straight. You tell him he goes in the spring. Then you tell him he goes in the winter and that he better get his affairs in order ASAP because the MAN says so and he WILL be in Alamogordo on his report date. Then you let the boy get married and pack all his stuff up in taped boxes, and then you tell him you have changed your mind and he will now report for camp in eight months and oh, by the way, you won't start paying him until he reports for camp. Well…thank you sir! We will make it work one damn way or the other because that is what mountain people do. Just yank our chain and we roll with it because that is what we do.

Elliott and Sydney were fine with the change. They were newlyweds after all and as long as they are together they are happy. The late report date was a problem for me. I had planned on riding triumphantly into Alamogordo in June to be greeted by my son who would see me riding into his city on my motorcycle, a modern day Alexander come to embrace his son. Now with his late report date I would ride into Alamogordo and no one would be there. Oh, there would be 15,000 or 20,000 people there, but none of them would be family so they might as well have been armadillos for all I cared. It's all about family for me.

As a mediator/lawyer, my schedule is firmly fixed months in advance. It took me scheduling the dates back in 2014 in order to have the June 3-20, 2015 dates on my calendar. There was no way to change them now and not lose a lot of revenue in my practice. I had reached one of those D-Day moments. I had to decide whether or not to go on the June 3-20 dates.

I spent several days mulling it over. If I waited until later in the summer and took the financial hit I would incur from taking another chunk out of my schedule, there would still be no guarantee the Air Force would not change his report date again. The weather would be problematic by late August and early September. The temperatures could be well over 100 for days on end. It would make for a tough trip. If I put the trip off now, I might never get it back on the calendar again and, unlike 30 years earlier, there was no guarantee I was going to live long enough to just put the trip off until "someday."

My mind was made up. I would go on June 3 and use the trip to explore Elliott's new home and report back to him and our family about what I had seen and what he and Sydney could expect when they went to his base.

So the Air Force had played calendar ping pong with our family and had hit squarely around, but never in the middle of my travel dates. The kids were happy and I had my date. I was still working on the route, but at least I knew when I was traveling. I was sure the Air Force would leave my trip alone from here on out. I was wrong. Later, much later in the trip, the Air Force gave a final set of orders that significantly impacted my plans one final time.

For now, though, I had my dates. I had my bike and I had more maps than Carter has liver pills. The route would come to me in time.

June 3, 2015 could not come soon enough.

Chapter 6

Day One

Headed West

There is an excitement, a giddy anticipation that precedes the taking of a much desired trip. It is like being a small child again on the night before Christmas. I had made my plans and packed my gear on the bike. I had been careful to pack light, taking only the bare minimum of clothing and ultralight backpacking camping gear. Everything I was carrying fit into my two aluminum panniers and a waterproof duffle strapped across the back of the bike. I had a tank bag strapped on top of the gas tank and used it to hold maps, batteries, headlamps, snacks, sunscreen, iPad, cell phone and the miscellaneous that just comes up on a trip. I would be in and out of that small bag many times every day during the trip and in the big luggage only once a day. My world was now very small and compact.

I had actually packed the bike several days before my start date just to be sure I had everything as close to perfect on the bike as possible. I would go out into the garage every morning when I got up to inspect the loaded bike and then repeat the process at night before going to bed. I have no idea what I thought would happen to all of my gear so tightly strapped to the bike, but I enjoyed checking it nonetheless.

I managed to get some sleep the night before I left and then I was up at six o'clock on June 3rd having breakfast, checking the weather and going over my straps and bags one last time. The weather was perfect, with clear skies, temperatures in the 70s and no wind. I was going to cover some serious ground today. My plan was to ride to Bowling Green before taking a break for fuel and to check my gear, then onto Paducah and after that, points west as far as I could go before the sun went down.

Susan was happy for me as we sat there having our morning coffee. She was not an enthusiastic endorser of the trip, but she was on board with seeing the plan through to success now that it was in motion. She had been that way on my trips to Africa and Alaska over the years to hunt and write articles for hunting journals. In some ways, I think she was more comfortable with me hunting Cape buffalo in Zimbabwe than she was with me riding a motorcycle across a very civilized America. Still, she was with me in spirit as my home base supporter and the remote logistics coordinator she would become as the trip unfolded. We finished our breakfast and I made my way down to the War Room one last time to gear up.

Adventure riders like me take their protective gear seriously. If there is such a thing as a safe motorcycle rider, then it is the adventure rider. The cruiser/Harley riders are all about black leather vests, sleeveless shirts, jeans and doo rags. Adventure riders are on the opposite end of the gear spectrum. I was seriously armored for the trip every day, even when temperatures soared to 105 degrees. Here is what I wore day in and day out:

- Full face adventure helmet
- Hard-shell armor upper body suit covering my arms, shoulders, chest, back and kidneys. I wore this under my coat.
- Aerostitch Hi-Viz yellow Gortex textile touring coat. It was absolutely waterproof, gave great crash protection for sliding on asphalt and was hot as an oven when not in motion. I never took it off.
- Aerostitch armored pants made of the same abrasion resistant, Gortex laminated fabric. They were also hot and they never came off when I was on the bike.
- Waterproof lace-up riding boots
- Neck gaiter, also known as a puff, to block the sun around my neck and the rain
- Leather gauntlet riding gloves
- CamelBak hydration system to keep me from dehydrating on long hot days. This proved to be an indispensable piece of equipment, much, much more important than the expensive German tool kit I carried on the trip and never used.

- Earplugs
- Lightweight hiking pants worn underneath the crash pants
- Lightweight shirts worn underneath the upper body armor
- Heavy wool socks to absorb perspiration and cool my feet
- Synthetic underwear
- Sunscreen

I wore all of that every second of every day I was on the bike. It may seem like a lot, but for me, I won't get on a bike without my gear. It's part of what makes the sport work for me. Riding a motorcycle is dangerous just like scuba diving and big game hunting, but participating in a dangerous activity does not mean one has to be suicidal in the undertaking, which is how I view the doo rag, leather vest riders. Do your thing your own way, but be prepared to face the consequences of your choices and don't ever ask anyone to foot the bill for your stupidity.

After I geared up, I walked to my bike, gave Susan one last kiss, posed for a few pictures and then I was on my way.

***   ***   ***   ***   ***

"I did it! I'm on my way! Alamogordo here I come!" I yelled those words over and over again as I began my ride on the four-lane parkway from London Road through Somerset headed west across Kentucky. This trip had been a year in the making and now it was happening. It was really happening! I was actually on my motorcycle and riding solo out west. I was alone and doing it on my own. I had lived to make the great adventure. I was leaving behind family who did not really want me to make this journey any more than they wanted me to fly to Africa and shoot buffalo years before, but they knew the doing of these things is who I was and who I was determined to remain even after the ravages of cancer. The essence of survival is to come out of the horror of the ordeal with at least some of who you are. This is what allows the survivor to claim the victory over the assailant, to look at the past and declare victory by still remaining upright on the battlefield. Wounded and battered, yes.

Defeated? Never.

I had been riding for about an hour when I realized I was going to pay for breaking one of the cardinal rules of adventure travel, which is to never make a substantive change in your gear within one month prior to the date of departure. I had a really nice custom saddle on my bike which was designed for 10-hour days on the road. I had encountered problems with it latching properly and I became concerned it would malfunction on the trip, so I ordered a mass market saddle for the bike which, according to all the glossy advertising in the motorcycle magazines, would give me the most comfortable ride in the history of the world.

Well, people in advertising lie. They just lie like dogs. The seat, which will remain nameless mostly because I don't want to be sued, was a torture device. I was burning and scooting around on the saddle before I made it to Bowling Green. I consoled myself by thinking the saddle would break in over time and that in just a few days I would be in that comfort zone promised by those advertising bastards on Madison Avenue or wherever it was they were hiding while they wrote their larcenous drivel. If there is an upside to a bad saddle, it is that the rider is motivated all the quicker to learn to ride standing up, which is something adventure bikes like mine were made for. By the time I made it to Paducah, I was riding standing up at highway speeds to give some relief to my backside, not to mention just enjoying the thrill of doing something that plain freaked out the old folks I passed on the interstate.

I think I must have looked like a big yellow banana as I moved on down the highway. Cool is not what adventure riders are after. We could care less how we look to people. Function is what we are all about and it is a high level of function we achieve with our unusual looking bikes and our spacesuit-type gear. It shields us from the elements and the insects that reside in them, and it protects us from the inevitable crashes and falls that go with the sport. Still, passing some goober driving a car while I was standing on the pegs at 75 mph put a smile on my face every time.

I had settled on a route that would take me through Paducah, Kentucky and on through southern Missouri and Kansas before turning south across the corners of Oklahoma and Texas and then into northeastern New Mexico. This route would keep me almost entirely off the interstate highways and give me the opportunity to see some of my country. One of the real benefits of motorcycle touring is the reconnection the rider can make with small town America, the kind of connection that was lost with the advent of the interstate highway system. If you need to get somewhere fast, then by all means take the interstate, clog your arteries with fries and cheeseburgers from the chains and stay in one bland hotel after another, meeting nothing more than one corporate image after another. If you want to see America, then get off the interstates and find America through the US Highway system or the even less traveled backroads. There you will find locally owned diners, greasy spoons, mom and pop motels and town squares where people actually live and transact business during the week. There was a time when that was America and people knew it for the familiar landscape it was no matter where we were in the country. There is a fear that pervades travel now. This is a fear of departure, a fear of leaving the comfortable, "get your miles on a credit card overnight stay and fly for free" mentality that has been inculcated in Americans like a sort of consumer catechism that drives profits to the bottom line for our retirement portfolios, but makes us all the more bland and ignorant of the people who share citizenship with us in this wonderful place called the United States of America. I was determined to find America again on my bike, no matter how dark and gloomy it appeared to others.

I had heard similar forecasts of doom, danger and death years before when I went to Africa to hunt buffalo with my friend, professional hunter Paul Ridgewell. Friends and family alike begged me not to go, so convinced were they I would never return from the Dark Continent. I would be killed by wild animals or robbed and murdered by bandits. In truth, any of that stuff could have happened, but it could also happen any time I am mediating a case in any of the American cities where I work or on one of my hikes in the bear and mountain lion infested forests of America. What I found in Africa were delightful people, funny people, brave people who would stand with me during a buffalo charge and just plain old ordinary, good people who wanted nothing more than to have a warm bed, someone to love and to wake up feeling safe and secure in the world as they knew it to be. If I could find that in Africa, then there stood at least a reasonable prospect I would find the same thing in America as I rode across the continent.

I wanted to let my family know what I was doing on the road. I wanted to share this experience, for good or for bad with them as I made my journey. I was carrying a mini-iPad with me with a small accessory keyboard. I had used it for over a year and I like to think I had become to some degree proficient in typing on the little thing. It was to become my means of communicating my adventure to my loved ones and to some of my biking buddies.

Unlike a lot of riders, I did not use a Bluetooth or any other device to channel music or sound of any kind into my helmet. I chose to ride with the environment and experience things as they came without a soundtrack. This was one of the best decisions I made on the trip. I had hours to think on the bike and the absence of music and phone calls kept my mind and attention free to experience and focus on the things that occurred as I rode. The ancillary, post-ride benefit at the end of the day was my increased desire for human contact and conversation. I developed a heightened sense for listening to the spoken word even when it was not directed at me.

At the end of each day, I wrote my travel log on my little iPad and emailed it out to my friends. What follows is each day's narrative exactly as I wrote it on the ride, bad grammar and all—just try writing on a six-inch keyboard with hands that are swollen and shaking from 10 hours in the saddle and you might appreciate my humble effort. (I begin Chapters 7 through 17 with these daily blog notes. These appear in italicized format before the chapter narratives, which are presented in traditional type.) I've added expanded comments to give perspective to each narrative, and in some places I've interrupted the narrative to provide further perspective to the transformative experience that was my life on the road.

The Caterpillar and his bike were on the way...

Chapter 7

Day One

Reflections

-----Original Message-----
From: Brian House
Sent: Wednesday, June 03, 2015 7:11 PM

I'm spending the night at the Honeysuckle Inn in tiny Mountain View, MO. I'm writing this from the little sports bar next door. Not sure why it's called a sports bar since there are no TVs and no sports memorabilia. It's also the only place to get something to eat. Kind of this town's version of Weavers. Folks are really nice.

I covered a lot of ground today—505 miles and would have done more, but I stopped twice to consult my maps. I'm a paper map guy even though my BMW comes with the most hi-tech GPS on earth. I just like to see the route before me and then ride it with some degree of confidence I know where I'm going. I had intended to camp tonight, but the campground I chose is 70 miles behind me so good was my progress today.

I covered familiar ground until I rode past the Oaks Mall in Paducah. After that it was new ground. Cairo, Illinois is an old, old river town that Susan and I are going to visit the next time we are down to visit her mother. There are many old buildings from the riverboat trade days there, including a U.S. Customs house.

The initial miles through southeast Missouri were flat farmland, but not the farmland of our youth. It's all massive, impersonal agribusiness. No Mom and Pop farms anymore. Kind of sad really.

I rode and am still riding U.S. 60. I had expected it to be a winding twisty two-laner. NO. It seems 60 is the major artery to suck tourists into Branson and the Ozarks. It's all four-lane and really nice. Just understand there's nothing there but forest and little towns, and I mean little towns.

My BMW did well today. I am able to ride it standing up which relieves my backside. I stood up off and on all day and was glad for the pegs under my body as opposed to the Harleys with the pegs way out in front of the rider.

Did I mention there are bugs out here? Yes, lots of them. Glad I am wearing a full face helmet and have a windscreen.

I ride to Coffeyville, Kansas tomorrow to visit the site of the Dalton Gang's demise. It was their last bank robbery. The townspeople rose up and fought back killing almost all of the gang. Some of the townspeople were killed in the shootout. I'll visit the museum and the Chamber of Commerce, which is located in the bank the Daltons tried to rob. Then it's onto western Kansas. I'll let you know where I am tomorrow night.

All is well and God is so very, very good.

Bless you all,
Brian

***   ***   ***   ***   ***

There are the plans you make and then there is the reality of the trip, the things that really happen on the road. I had thought I would stop at one campground only to find I was making better time than I had planned for so I kept on going. This did two things: it put me further along my journey across the Midwest and it opened the door for more discovery as I was now stopping in places I had not researched prior to departure.

Paducah, Kentucky was my point of departure for parts unknown. I had first practiced law in Paducah after graduating from law school and some of my wife's family still lives there so it was all familiar to me. Crossing the river into Cairo, Illinois was another world. Cairo of Mark Twain fame must have been a grand river city back when Huckleberry Finn was being written. The old U.S. Customs House is still there in all its imposing federal glory, but that's about it. The town was little more than tired streets and vacant buildings. The course of America's commerce was headed in different directions those days. I had refueled in Paducah so I rode through Cairo without giving it a thorough look, so it is entirely possible my comments have not done justice to the place, but I was on the main road and I saw what the community leaders saw fit to offer folks who drive that route. The line of sight vision of the motorcycle traveler is the entire world to those of us who see the world looking out from a tight helmet while on the road.

I spent the remainder of the day on really nice smooth asphalt four-lane connector roads which appeared to have been built to funnel tourists into the vacation mecca of the Ozark Mountains and Branson, Missouri. The natural beauty of the green rolling mountains of the region was easily appreciated, as was the lack of people. Just not a lot of folks there and certainly not a town of any real size, all of which is perfect for a motorcycle traveler who just wants to be on the road. As my day wound down, I had to make plans for the night and because I was making good time my plans were changing fast.

I found the Honeysuckle Inn by consulting my iPad late in the day when I made a gas stop. It was clear I was going to ride beyond the campground I had planned on using, so I had to find another one, only...there wasn't another for hundreds of miles along my route. I had planned on camping a lot on this trip and here I was on the first night out and it was looking like a hotel night.

***   ***   ***   ***   ***

The Honeysuckle's website sold itself as a locally owned, clean and happy place for travelers who were Ozark-bound and maybe on their way to and from Branson, the country music venue of the Midwest, also known as the place where careers come to die. I would not be going to Branson, but I would be staying at the dear old Honeysuckle.

The motel was located on my westbound left in tiny

Mountain View and it was situated below grade in a busy little area such that you would miss the place if you were not looking for it. I missed it on my first pass, but made a quick turnaround and pulled in. The lady at the desk was the owner and she was used to bikers. She cheerily showed me to my first floor room on the front which afforded me a parking space in front of my door and told me to let her know if I had any problems. I turned the AC on full blast and started unloading my bike. I was at the end of my first solo day on the road.

     ***   ***   ***   ***   ***

You are never really alone on the road, or at least you are only as lonely as you want to be. There were four really nice touring motorcycles parked at the Honeysuckle when I pulled in. They were the Honda Goldwing variety, massive machines and immaculately maintained. Like my bike, each one was adorned with a decal or two that conveyed a message about the travel history and life experiences of their owners. From these little markers, I deduced these guys were veterans from back east. They were on the road like me.

The Goldwingers, as I called them, were standing outside their rooms adjacent to mine when I walked by. We greeted each other and then I headed straight for the shower to cool off and relax a bit before dinner. I had brought no real off-the-bike clothes for the trip, just a pair of extra hiking pants and a few extra t-shirts. I changed into fresh clothes and made my way to what the diary above refers to as the sports bar that wasn't a sports bar.

Misnomers abound on the road and that's part of the fun of the thing, the hilarity of the obvious local folks never appreciate because they have seen it so much they are desensitized to the nonsense of it all. A sports bar without televisions and no sports pics, no memorabilia hanging on the wall. How could it be a sports bar? Well, it had the one essential ingredient needed for such an establishment: beer, ice cold almost frozen in the bottle beer. Yes, as far as I was concerned, the place was a sports bar. I ordered from a very limited menu of the everything-but-the-salads-are-fried variety, took a long drink from my beer and settled back to think and write my blog before my salad came. There were a few people in the place doing, from what I could tell, exactly what I was doing, relaxing after a day on the road and not really giving a damn about the lack of a sports bar inside.

Every traveler has his own individual points of reference, the things that provide perspective, giving a lens of analysis to the trip. At the beginning of the trip, I think it is most often the things from home that we refer to as we encounter things on the road. In the blog I mentioned Weaver's, which was a short order restaurant that had existed in my hometown for decades before burning to the ground the winter before I left for the ride. It had been a local institution, the kind of place with a "Liar's Table" where the old codgers gathered every day to throw forth their opinions on the world's problems. The food was unique with a secret chili for their "chili buns" and the place was absolutely indispensable to understanding the little town of London because it was there that folks came to see old friends and strangers came to view all the photographs and memorabilia of historic London that adorned the walls of the place. To look at the walls of Weaver's was to gain some insight into how my hometown had come to be as seen through the eyes of the all the amateur photographers who had donated photos to the succession of proprietors of Weaver's. There was a photograph of me sitting on a shelf, and when it went up in flames on Super Bowl 2015, part of me went up in flames with it. Still, my memories of going there since I was a child are part of who I am, and when I walk into a place like I did in Mountain View, the old memories are stirred and I am both at the sports bar and back home at the same time.

***   ***   ***   ***   ***

Riding a motorcycle long distances is a very tiring undertaking. Touring motorcycles are substantial machines. My bike weighed about 600 pounds fully loaded, which is a real lightweight as far as touring bikes go. It felt light in motion, but it still took effort to throw the thing around on the highway and real leg strength to move it around in a parking lot. A long day in the saddle is a real workout, especially in hot weather. By the time I made it to the sports bar next door to the Honeysuckle Inn, I had certainly registered my workout for the day. I finished my meal and my blog and made the short walk across the grass of the shared yard between the two establishments back to the motel where I stopped in at the front desk before going to my room.

The elderly proprietor told me her son is the co-owner of the place and is a truck driver who is on the road down in Texas, but will be back in a few days to "check on things." I don't know if she offered this to me as reassurance the place was being well looked after or just conversation, but I took it for what it was and told her my story of being on the road to Alamogordo. She suggested I post a review on one of the travel sites since things like that help her business. I told her I would as soon as I had time to do so.

The next morning, I was up early and loaded my bike for the day's ride. It was a nomad's existence with my home being my bike and not the places where I stopped. The other bikers were doing the same thing and it wasn't long before we struck up a conversation. They were on their way north to ride the narrow, curvy backroads of the Midwest and to ride as many of them as possible before arriving at Sturgis, South Dakota to see the town a month in advance of the famous annual bikers rally. These guys were all retired factory workers, teachers and ex-military. One of them saw the "Air Force Dad" sticker on my bike and asked me about my son. I explained to them about my trip to his base at Alamogordo. Another rider, a burly fellow sporting a full gray beard and wearing a Vietnam veterans cap came up to me and extended his hand saying, "Tell him we thank him for his service." It was all I could do not to break down on the spot because I knew they understood his sacrifice and service. So many times I hear those words from people who have made the conscious decision to never serve and to do all they can to see to it that their children run like hell from service. I find those words coming from people like that to be offensive as I worry about my son's safety and grieve his absence from my life. Coming from these fellows, though, was another matter. I treasured those words as one of the highlights of my trip.

***   ***   ***   ***   ***

With every highlight I suppose comes some balance, a lowlight if you will, to keep the karma in the thing. I found mine at the Honeysuckle when I woke up that morning and started getting dressed.

Bedbugs. The Honeysuckle Inn had bedbugs. I never knew if

it was just my room that was infested or was it the whole place. I did not hear the Goldwing guys complaining as we all loaded up that morning so maybe it was just my room. Still, I had the raised red whelps that are the markers of bedbug bites and I actually picked one of the little bastards off my waist as I was getting dressed. I was missing my tent as I thought of the possibility of all my gear being infested on day one. The good news for me was the intense heat generated in my aluminum panniers and enclosed bags would kill any hobo bedbugs and that was in fact what happened. I never had another bedbug on the trip, but I did have the bite marks and whelps as a reminder of my stay at the Honeysuckle.

If you look for my review of this little inn on a travel website, you won't find it. I did the little old lady a favor and gave her a pass on the bedbug thing. I figured it wouldn't be long before some really irate individual of the Samuel L. Jackson in *Pulp Fiction* variety would come storming into her lobby after a night in my old room and go medieval on her. My guess is the bedbug thing was fumigated away in short order. Either that or the place is out of business. One can only hope.

There is good and there is not so good on the road. You just have to keep a sense of humor about things. I always wondered what the whole bedbug thing was about and now I know. I can chalk it up to another of my great life experiences I never want to repeat. That and the stale waffle the Honeysuckle called breakfast that morning. Still, it got me on down the road which is what I was after anyway.

One day and one night of travel had seen me leave my home, ride across Kentucky, through Illinois for just a few minutes and then deep into Missouri. I was well on my way now, far off the beaten path and certainly far away from luxury accommodations. Yes, it was misnamed bars, bedbugs and stale waffles, but it was also the grand old river town of Cairo and the rolling hills of the Ozarks. It was my bike racking up the miles without a complaint and it was me doing it all, soaking everything in for better or for worse. I was living the experience, making it my adventure on my terms.

It was time to head to Kansas.

Chapter 8

Day Two

We're in Kansas, Toto

-----Original Message-----
From: Brian House
Sent: Thursday, June 04, 2015 10:25 PM

I covered 450 miles today. The early morning miles—about 200 through western Missouri and eastern Kansas—were sunshine, some early fog and farmland. The afternoon miles were really hard— crosswinds that threw me all over the place and hammered my head senseless for three hours. I passed a wind farm that went for miles to the horizon and just kept going. There had to be over a thousand wind propellers turning.

I travelled backroads mostly today. Just 40 miles of interstate. Some of the things I saw today:

Dead armadillos: the little fellows are all over the place. They make a prettier corpse than their cousins the opossums, but they are just as dead.

Pecan groves: Kansas State University is growing large groves of pecans in what appears to be flooded bottoms. There were white egrets all over the place. Reminded me of the ocean.

I rode through a little village that had a sign posted by a bar that read "Coors Lite Welcomes You," and then not 100 feet later another sign: "God Loves You". Make of it what you will.

I rode through Sharon, Kansas, the home of Martina McBride. I can

---

see why she left.

I had lunch at "Big G's" in tiny Caney, Kansas. Big G was wearing a camo shirt that almost covered his ample belly and topped it off with a well-worn camo hat. His wife fried my potatoes. She had calves that makes Lance Armstrong's legs look like weenies. While I was eating at one of the tables outside, a toothless cowboy came up to me and struck up a conversation. People always want to know where I'm going. When I told him I was riding to western Kansas, he shook his head and said, "I'm sorry. That place is just a damn desert like New Mexico." I told him I was going to ride all over New Mexico. He said he worked there for two years recently and didn't see more than 10 rattlesnakes the entire time. Big G gave him his order and toothless cowboy said goodbye. As he drove away he stuck his head out the window and yelled, "Watch out for rattlesnakes!" I'm sleeping in a hotel tonight.

I stopped twice to look at maps today to make sure I was going the way I intended. I stopped another time when one of my alert messages came on. The "check oil" light came on late in the afternoon. I called BMW Roadside assistance. The nice BMW man told me they don't help you fix anything, they just pick up their nonworking crap and haul it to a dealer. Marvelous. I then called my local dealer in Louisville and talked to the head of the service department. He is why there should never be legalized marijuana sales in Kentucky. I explained my problem to him and he said, "Wow man. I haven't seen that on the new bikes. Just a couple have been brought in that just died and don't run anymore and, what do you know, we've been totally, like, slammed here today man and, like, my technician is gone for the day, and so I'm sorry. And hey man, why don't you get it checked out and let me know what 'they' tell you." So, I did what Matt House's grandson should have done in the first place: I checked the bike. Oil level was fine, no leaks, all seals solid. I let the bike sit for 30 minutes, started it and it ran fine. I'm taking it to the Santa Fe BMW dealer while I'm out here to get it checked. I figure they smoke a classier brand of dope in Santa Fe so they should really give it a going over.

I have seen more dead deer than I can count. Kansas is covered up with deer. I'm not riding early or late because of those little guys.

Being a preacher, I've been keeping a tally of the kinds of churches. The Baptists and the Christian Churches (both independents and Disciples of Christ) pretty much have it to themselves. There are Catholic churches and the occasional Lutheran, but that's about it. When I get to New Mexico, I'll be faced with the dilemma of whether to add the New Age Crystal people into my church tally.

Tomorrow I will ride out of Western Kansas and into northeastern New Mexico. It will take me about seven hours to get to Eagle Nest, NM. I am going to spend the night there at the Laguna Vista Lodge so I can visit what True West Magazine calls the best bar in the west. After that I will make my way to Santa Fe and then we'll see.

Finally, I will note that it is hot as Satan's Hell out here. I rode for hours in temperatures of mid-90s. I wear full body armor, crash pants and coat along with a full face helmet and gauntlet gloves. I really don't get hot, but I stay thirsty. I would not be able to make it without my CamelBak.

That will do it for tonight.

> *Be safe everyone and watch out for rattlesnakes,*
> *Brian*

***   ***   ***   ***   ***

How do I say this and be polite about it? Let's see...here it goes. The wind in Kansas is a bitch. That about sums it for the truth and honesty part of the riding conditions. Add to that the oppressive Kansas flatland heat that was totally unremitting and you have my summary of the weather. It would be easy to just stop there and launch into a rant on the wind, but that would be unfair to what was really a fun day once I got past the wind pushing my bike all over the place. My Kansas adventure took unexpected turns right from the start.

   I left the Huckleberry Inn at about 7:30 that morning and rode with the early morning sun comfortably at my back. It was blue skies with just an occasional cloud or two and no wind. I thought I had dodged the famous prairie winds, but they were just waiting for me out there later in the afternoon. My morning destination was Coffeyville, Kansas, the site of the infamous Dalton bank robbery which took place on October 5, 1892. I am an Old West buff and have made many trips over the years to visit the ghost towns and still thriving communities of the West where history was made. I try to spend a few weeks every year in Arizona or New Mexico, just soaking up the history of places like Tombstone, Bisbee, Nogales, Las Vegas, New Mexico, the Badlands of South Dakota and the Little Big Horn in Montana, to name a few. It just seemed right that I would make a stop in tiny Coffeyville and take in the site of the town's courageous defense against the infamous Dalton's, who were more or less wiped out by a well-armed and determined populace.

Riding across a continent puts distance on a map in serious perspective. What looks like an insignificant distance on a paper map unfolded in your lap can turn into hours of hard riding. A rider is constantly calculating the distance traveled and the time remaining in the day to continue the ride. It is easier to make these calculations if you just have a direction and not a destination. I was bound for Alamogordo, which was two hard days of riding away if I kept up a ride-all-day pace. There would be just enough time to cruise down a rustic western street and dismount to walk along preserved storefronts or have a piece of pie (no beer while riding) at a cafe and buy a souvenir and move on. The signs to Coffeyville were clearly marked, and the closer I got the more billboards I saw advertising various businesses in the Coffeyville area. Prosperity it seems, or some small measure of it, had made its way to Coffeyville in the years since the townsfolk killed Grat Dalton, Bob Dalton, Dick Broadwell and Bill Power, while the outlaws killed four defenders. All this prosperity had apparently culminated in some sort of community patriotic celebration on the day I rode into town. Streets were blocked off and traffic was directed away from the part of town I wanted to see. American flags were flying everywhere as was red, white and blue bunting. Perhaps it was a political rally or the coming home of a local hero from afar, I will never know. It became apparent the only way I would get to the robbery site would be to park my bike blocks away and leave it unguarded while I trudged to town center wearing my armored suit in 90-degree weather.

I parked, thought about it for a minute and decided visiting the site of the Dalton gang's demise would have to wait until another day. I did not mind walking in the heat, but leaving my bike parked out of my sight was a recipe for disaster and I did not want to chance losing any of my gear at such an early point in the trip. It was time for me to be on the road.

It's the incongruity of what you see when you travel that gives the color to the trip. Prior to crossing the Kansas border, I had envisioned the entire state to be just part of the endless wheat fields of the great American breadbasket. I was certain I would be riding through amber waves of grain along with the occasional white farmhouse standing majestically in the distance. I am sure those places were there, but not on the southern route I took through the state. There was a lot of agriculture, but it looked a lot like western Kentucky to me. Still lots of green yards and plenty of trees with deer everywhere. Fortunately, all of the deer I saw were very dead, which is a good thing for motorcyclists since hitting a deer is one of our greatest fears. I appreciated the cars and trucks which had done their best to thin the herd before I got there.

Who knew there were armadillos as far north as Kansas? I am sure plenty of people did, but I was not one of them. There they were, these armored corpses littering the sides of the road breaking up the monotony over me seeing the dead deer decorate the ditch lines. Maybe they have always been there, but it was news to me. I thought about the little guys as I rode and I wondered why Kansas had not made the armadillo its state animal. I mean, it's an armored marsupial and a pretty mean looking little dude at that. He would make a great collegiate mascot except for the beady eyes, but put a football helmet on him and he would be good to go. Why weren't diners serving armadillo burgers or armadillo dogs? It could work. We have been talked into eating pigs, and if you have ever seen where a pig lives then you will know it's possible to market anything and convince people it is clean enough to eat it. Just tell people something often enough, long enough and they will get used to it.

Such was surely the case when I rode through the little village with the "Coors Lite" and "God loves you" signs. They weren't a hundred yards apart. I envisioned a fundamentalist Pentecostal, King James Bible in one hand and his hammer in the other, erecting the "God Loves You" sign while his ne'er-do-well bartender brother, beer in one hand, was erecting the "Coors Lite" sign just to piss his brother off. Enough time had passed and now the signs coexisted within comfortable eyesight of one another and life went on in the small town. I like to think the bartender was also a Pentecostal who tithed. If he gave enough, I doubt they would turn him down.

I rode past the few houses that constituted Martina McBride's neighborhood and was through it in the blink of an eye. Such a tiny spot on the side of the road and they sure loved their girl! The sign they had honoring her was a billboard that was well maintained. It was about lunchtime when I rolled past her billboard so I started looking for a place to eat. Signs eventually pointed me to the town of Caney, Kansas, and it was there I hit the jackpot when I found "Big G's," a classic white concrete block hamburger stand with six indoor seats and two picnic tables outside in the shade. The place just had locals written all over it. There were three pickup trucks parked in the parking lot as well as a motorcycle. These were my kind of people so my lunch plans were made.

I learned early on that people could see the fatigue on my face. I don't know if it was the heat or just the time in the saddle, but I sure engendered a lot of compassionate behavior from folks. I ordered my food and went outside to strip off the armor and cool down some. I more or less just collapsed onto the picnic table and started studying my maps. A few minutes later, Big G himself walked outside with my burger and fries and told me he could tell I was tired. Turns out he was a biker and rode his Harley to work when he could. My view of Harley guys improved considerably from that day forward.

I make my living mediating day in and day out with lawyers and trained claims professionals. Our conversations are governed by the language of our profession and the laws which apply to the particular case at hand. I love what I do and I really enjoy the people I meet practicing law as a mediator. Still, our conversations are regimented and disciplined, and while intellectually stimulating because they are goal-oriented, they just don't have the color and flavor of talking to the toothless cowboy who told me New Mexico was "just a damn desert." In my everyday life, I wear suits and ties which a lot of people find off-putting. I sure don't have a lot of working people coming up to me in restaurants in Lexington or

Louisville and talking to me. But out here, beaten down by the wind and the heat, wearing my armor and heavy boots, a cowboy with no teeth and driving a worn out pickup truck felt comfortable enough to come up to me and strike up a conversation. Strip away the appearance of wealth and the privilege of professional station and people become ordinary again, just talk and get to know one another. If I had been sitting there in my business suit and my black dress shoes, I think the cowboy would not have spoken to me because he would have thought I thought I was better than him. He would have been wrong about me, but the damage would have been done and we would have never spoken to each other. We would have missed the opportunity to pass a pleasant conversation in a tiny town in Kansas eating a fine burger prepared by Big G himself. I'm glad my business suit was left at home.

I had made a really good trade opting out of the gift shops of Coffeyville and choosing Big G's for my midday break. Now it was time to move on and ride into central Kansas. I was aiming for Medicine Lodge, another community on the map that was just a name to me, but it would be my destination to end the day's ride. It was my hope there would either be a campground or a hotel there for the night. It was early afternoon when I left Big G's behind and rode out on the backroads into rural Kansas.

Rural backroads should not be interpreted to mean narrow one-lane roads with flowers growing on the side and Jersey milk cows contentedly munching away on their cuds. The Kansas backroads were busy two-lane paved affairs with extensive passing lanes built in and placed apart by several miles. I wondered why this infrastructure was there since agriculture could not account for all of the road development. My maps certainly did not give away the extent of the infrastructure. Then they began passing me and I began meeting some going the other way. Tractor trailers hauling what at first seemed to be massive fins perhaps 75-feet-long and 10-feet-high. It was certainly a piece of high-tech equipment and then I saw their purpose in action on the horizon. There were wind turbines, thousands of them spread out before me on the Kansas plain.

It is an eerie thing to see so many artificial giants in motion on the ancient, prehistoric horizon of the prairie. The land that had been essentially undisturbed for millennia was now covered with these wind turbines rising hundreds of feet into the air helping to meet our country's insatiable thirst for ever more energy to power all the things we now deem necessary and essential to our lives.

These giant beasts should have been a clue, a big, spinning tip-off to the hell that was waiting up ahead for me, but I remained oblivious to the invisible threat that lay out there. The afternoon sun was beating down steadily on my head when I leaned into a curve making a long, gradual sweeping change of direction. Without warning, I was suddenly lifted off my bike while it was pushed sideways into the oncoming lane of travel. I had been totally unprepared for my first greeting from the Kansas wind. I recovered quickly and launched into what would become a long two-day battle with the wind. There was some respite on this, the first of my two hardest days, but the wind was there to pop up and hit me over and over again, never really going away with the result that I was tense and on the hyper alert for another burst. I certainly did not get sleepy on this leg of the journey. I just kept the throttle turned and leaned into the wind all the while grateful for such a solid bike to get me through.

Then the warning lights came on.

Warning lights should never light up on a brand new motorcycle, particularly one that is so expensive you don't want your wife to ever, ever know what you paid for the damn thing, and if she finds out like mine did, you fall back on the argument that the Germans have made this thing and it's as perfect to God's creation as the hand of man can possibly make and it will get me through all of this alive and never let me down and aren't you glad I was thinking of you when I laid out all this cash to protect our future?

Well, it sounded better when I made the argument at home. Now, riding down the road at 60 mph, seeing the "Check Oil" and "Warning Engine Temperature" lights come on while doing battle with the great winds of the North West was almost too much to handle. Still, I had spent the extra money on the service plans and BMW owner associations and warranty plans and all that would get me through. Except that they did not. They failed miserably.

While I make light of the spaced out BMW people I spoke with over the phone, they really were that bad. It was pointless to get mad at them over the phone. I mean, what good would it have possibly done to scream into a phone at the little gas station in the middle of Kansas with wind whipping around me so bad I had to throw my coat over my head so I could hear the phone? All of that roadside assistance is great if you live in a major metropolitan area, but if you are a cross country rider then having a problem with your fancy BMW means you are just on your own and you had better grow yourself a monstrous pair and get yourself out of it.

I ended up using common sense and drew upon some of what I remember my late father doing when we worked on engines in my childhood. In the end, I inspected my machine and made the decision it was road-worthy in spite of the little computers and lights the Germans had stuck on the engine to make it more marketable. Boiled down to its essentials, my motorcycle was still just a combustion engine and that technology has really not changed in 75 years. If it doesn't leak and it has fuel and coolant, it should get you down the road which is exactly what happened. I rode without incident to Medicine Lodge and found an inexpensive room for the night. It was a really tiny community. My food options were the pizza the guy in the gas station was heating up or something ordered curbside at the local Sonic drive-in. I opted for the Sonic experience, ordered a grape Slushee and a grilled chicken sandwich and sat there watching the life of another classic Midwestern village wind down for the day.

I sat outside the Sonic at one of those circular metal table chair combos that are dipped in plastic and are not terribly comfortable for anyone to use and more so for a tired biker whose backside was very unhappy with his new saddle. I took my time to watch the cars and pickups pull in and out of the drive-in. Most people were ordering ice cream, which made perfect sense to me on such a hot day. There was no shade where the Sonic owners had placed the table, so I was more or less baking while I had my rubber chicken sandwich.

"What would the people who made history in this town think of Medicine Lodge now?" I wondered.

Medicine Lodge, Kansas has always been a small community. It has about 2,000 people in it and that number is dropping as the years go by. The place gets its name from the medicine lodge erected nearby by the Kiowa people as part of their celebration of their annual sun dance in 1866. The area was considered sacred by the Kiowa due to their discovery of Epsom salts in the Medicine Lodge River. Treaties were signed there in 1867. White settlers founded the town proper in 1873. When the

Indian wars escalated in 1874, a stockade was built. A reproduction of the stockade now stands in Medicine Lodge and is open to the public.

Medicine Lodge was also the place where a lot of lives were ruined or saved, depending on your perspective, and where the seeds for organized crime were sown in a very unintentional way. Little old Carrie Nation launched her hatchet-wielding crusade against alcohol here in 1920 while she was living in the place. Those of us who enjoy Kentucky bourbon just wish she would have stayed home.

It's hard to get a hold of all that history and the people like the great chiefs, Carrie Nation and the anonymous pioneers who have, at various times, called this little place home. That's how so many communities are across America. You ride through a town and all you see are the buildings and the signs and maybe someone walking down the sidewalk if there is a sidewalk. But it takes stopping and spending time with people to really get a grasp for why the place exists and why it matters to the people who call it home. My journey to New Mexico would not permit me time to do that sort of exploring here, but it would be the way I would let the Land of Enchantment unfold around me.

We Americans pick all kinds of places in which to live out our lives. Yes, there are some spectacular places, but we can't all live in Jackson Hole or Lake Tahoe. Some of us live in little London, Kentucky or tiny Medicine Lodge, Kansas, and it is in those places we fall in love, raise our children, grow old and die. Along the way, we do our best to contribute to our communities and make our little towns function. I like to think every person who chooses to work adds something to a town that is essential and will be missed when they are gone. A garbage collector and a lawyer are of equal necessity in the life of a community. Some might say the garbage man is more so. A housewife and a surgeon are equally important to the social construct of an orderly and well-functioning community. People like Big G and the toothless cowboy make life richer and well worth the effort it took to get there and meet them. All it took was my time and a smile, and my life was made forever better by letting them come into my life.

I ended Day Two reflecting on those chance encounters and these wonderful little towns no one has ever heard of. I had hoped for all the dots on my map to be checked off in an orderly manner, but it was now apparent to me that was not going to happen. I was still in my cocoon trying to understand what being a survivor is all about and here came the random and the unpredictable, but this time it was good. It was all good.

With luck and a functioning motorcycle, it was my plan to reach New Mexico the next day.

Luck and hopefully a lot less wind.

Chapter 9

Day Three

Into New Mexico

-----Original Message-----

From: Brian House
Sent: Friday, June 05, 2015 11:09 PM

I made it to Eagle Nest, New Mexico today. It was a long 475-mile ride, but I got here. I saw some really beautiful terrain today interspersed among some horrific Kansas wind and an hour-long thunder and lightning storm on the way to Taos. All told I have ridden 1,430 miles these past three days.

First, the good stuff:

I left a thoroughly forgettable motel in Medicine Lodge, Kansas and rode through the Gypsum Hills Scenic Area of western Kansas on highway 160. The fields were lush green and flowers were everywhere. The road is mile after mile of rollers that are straight as a ruler. Within 20 miles of leaving Medicine Lodge, the terrain began to look like the real West or at least what I think it looks like with grazing land for as far as the eye can see. There were some wheat crops growing, but they soon gave way to beef ranches.

I had lunch today at a tiny Mexican restaurant about 25 miles from the Kansas/Texas border. The food was excellent. I was the only customer. There was a "For Sale" sign in the window. I suspect I was one of the last patrons.

Then came the bad stuff:

The winds today were the worst I've ever ridden in. Granted, there are a lot of riders with many more years of experience, but I'll just say I leaned and pushed and pulled for all I was worth to keep the GS pointed in the right direction. This little wind gauntlet lasted for two hours. It was all I ever wanted of that particular fresh hell and I'll be looking for a different return route home.

The winds finally begin to abate after I left Oklahoma and rode into Texas. It was really hard for me to find a direct route road with low traffic numbers. Every road I picked had a stated speed limit of 65 or 70 or 75, which meant trucks were flying. Each one punished me with a blast. I was thrilled to cross the Texas/New Mexico state line and I thought I was home free.

The road to Eagle Nest is essentially the road to Taos from an eastern approach. You can see the mountains in the distance. They are majestic and for me signaled my arrival. The only problem was the massive storm brewing on top of those mountains. The closer I rode, the more lightning and thunder came my way. I hoped it would go around, but no such luck. The full force of the storm hit me and stayed with me for 50 miles. I got it all from wind, rain, tiny hail, lightning and pooled water on the road. Since there is no place to ever pull off to the side of the roads out west, it was either ride and maybe die or stop in the road and die for sure. I rode. I am really pleased with the GS. I put it in Road/Wet mode and the bike performed great. I rounded a curve to find a huge puddle covering the entire road. The GS went through it like it was dry ground. My Aerostitch coat and pants were rock solid waterproof as well.

Now for my major disappointment: I rode to Eagle Nest to visit the Laguna Vista bar which has been called by some "The Best Bar In The West." That's a pretty tall order when you think of the Crystal Palace in Tombstone or one of several bars in Bisbee, AZ or the bar at the Erma Hotel. The Laguna bar had no draft beers of any kind. It did have a few pool tables of the put-your-quarters-in variety. When I went in there at 8:30, there wasn't a soul in the place. The gas station attendant told me tomorrow is "Fish For Free" day in New Mexico and everyone is home getting their tackle ready. I asked her what the big fish around these parts was and she replied "bluegill, but they are bigger this year." There you have it. Next time you want someone to quit drinking just take them bluegill fishing. Works every time.

The road from I-25 Exit 486 to Eagle Nest is just absolutely, stunningly awesome. Curves and curves and curves with streams rolling alongside the road and antelope grazing nearby. I counted 14 of the little lopesters. Think of this stretch of road as being similar to the Dragon, but three times as long with much better scenery. That, of course, is why I really made the journey to the mountain.

I'm going to dial down the miles tomorrow and get some rest. I am more than a little tired.

Bless you all,
Brian

***   ***   ***   ***   ***

Life on the road exhibits a kind of choreography, a cadence of repetition when traveling for days on end. By day three, my little ballet of the road had taken shape. I would wake up early and start the process of repacking the liner bags which held my gear inside the aluminum panniers on the bike. There is a discipline to packing correctly for motorcycle travel. The weight must first balance the bike. The bike starts off unbalanced for luggage purposes because there is a large muffler on one side which has to be compensated for by the luggage/panniers when they are installed. This is accomplished by making the muffler side pannier smaller than the other side's pannier. From that point on, the weight of the internal bags must be the same. Getting the weight right at home was easily accomplished by standing on scales with each bag and arriving at a more or less equal weight distribution. On the road it is less precise and is further complicated by packing according to the contents. You don't want to pack camping gear and stove fuel with clothing and video gear unless you want to smell like a stove and have no camera for the rest of the trip when a leak spoils the contents of the bag. I ended up packing camping gear, tools and fuel on the muffler side and the lighter, more numerous things on the larger pannier side. The weight balanced.

Once you have the weight distributed, the weight must then be placed low and forward in each bag. This centers the weight toward the bike's lowest point of gravity, which makes it handle better. One of the reasons my bike handles so well is the low center of gravity created by the odd-looking boxer style engine, which places the bulk of the engine's weight at the absolute bottom of the frame. This makes for an unusual sight compared to the big vertically mounted, slender V-twin engines Americans are accustomed to seeing on Harleys and other cruiser style bikes. The boxer engine, though odd to some in appearance, is super reliable and exhibits that super low center of gravity, which makes it perfect for adventure travel and the varying terrains these bikes were designed for. When a touring rider takes care to keep the panniers packed equal, low and forward, then the bike will handle smoothly on the road and the weight will not be noticed during riding. Packing correctly then became my first order of the day every day because doing it right meant there was one less thing to worry about when I put the bike in gear and headed out on the road.

Once the panniers were loaded, I then strapped on the waterproof duffle, also known as a "Dry Bag," onto the back of the bike. I carried my tent, sleeping bag, air mattress and some clothing in this bag. It was held onto the bike by several straps and cords, which I tightened down until the bag would not shift or move. A shifting bag on a motorcycle in motion guarantees a wreck and can be avoided by careful work. I knew exactly where my straps went on the bike every day and the order in which they were tightened down. It was a time-consuming process, but it worked without fail. All of this had to be done rain or shine no matter the heat or the cold, shade or blazing sun. It was part of life on the road and I became very comfortable with that morning routine.

I did all of this before I left the motel in Medicine Lodge. It was a worn out affair with stray cats everywhere. The little beggars had clearly started life at this place and would end their existence there one way or the other. They tried getting in my room the night before, and when I denied them entry they hung around outside my door meowing for food and just generally waiting to dash in the door if I gave them the chance. All I could think of was a flea infestation to cap off the bedbug attack from the night before. Eventually the little guys grew tired of me and went on to torment a fracking worker who was staying in a room on the opposite side of the parking lot.

Fracking workers became a familiar sight for me, as did the fracking rigs that are now all over the West. This form of oil production is a really emotional topic out west. Proponents argue fracking brings high paying jobs and economic prosperity to an area that needs them and will make life better with no harm to the environment. It should come as no surprise that lots of ranchers and environmentalists disagree. They point to the increase in seismic disturbances and the dropping water tables in the region. Ranchers fear the frackers will ruin the water and leave the land an arid desert when the frackers move on their way like devouring locusts. It is rumored there have been violent confrontations between these groups. I rarely saw a fracker's truck with any kind of logo on the side, but they were easy to spot because they were the newest three-fourths-ton pickups on the road. Ranchers drove older and dirtier trucks. I suspect the ranchers could spot the fracker trucks much easier than could I. One thing I came to appreciate was the fracker's crew boss picking out clean hotels. If I saw fracker trucks in the parking lot of a motel, then I knew it had been checked out and was clean because those guys worked in the same places over and over again and would have no interest in being eaten alive by bedbugs every night. Their business was a real boon to these out-of-the-way motels, which meant the owners had an incentive to keep them clean and earn the return business of these itinerant crews. Don't misunderstand me, these motels were still rough $30-a-night affairs with beds covered in thin linens, flat pillows, a shower and little else, but they were free of bedbugs and fleas and had air conditioning, which was enough for men on the road.

I made some coffee in the in-room coffee maker and enjoyed a Styrofoam cup of the bitter brew before getting on the bike. There was no place to eat breakfast in Medicine Lodge, so I rode west planning on a big lunch. The little tribe of cats was zeroing in on the open door of the fracker's truck as I pulled out of the parking lot.

The sky was incredibly blue as I pulled the clutch in with my left hand and lifted my left foot up against the gear shifter, working my way through the first five gears of the bike while picking up speed on the road heading west away from town. There was no traffic to speak of at this early hour. My route was going to take me through the Gypsum Hills Scenic Area today and I, of course, had no idea what that meant. It could have been a gravel pile for all I knew. What mattered to me was the route took me to New Mexico.

There are times when wonderful things, life-defining things, epic moments rise up and occur without any warning. This happened as I rode into the Gypsum Hills. This area can best be described as having the same colors and earthen tones as the red rock country of Sedona, Arizona and the Georgia O'Keefe environs of northern New Mexico, but with lots of pastureland to go with them. The red and orange hues of the land were stunning with the soft light of the early morning sun bathing each distant, open expanse as my bike took me up and down the gently rolling knobs of the area. This was cattle country for the most part and the grazing pastures were neon green in June. Later in the summer they would dry out and become a brittle brown, but I rode through on a day when the land was perfect. I raised my helmet visor and let the sweet air of the grass pastures blow in. I decided not to be in a hurry and slowed down and let the miles roll by at a pace that would make any Sunday driver proud. This was beautiful country devoid of commercial structure; the frackers had not found it, or more likely had, concluded there was no oil underneath and moved on. Their defeat in finding oil had preserved this pristine area. All of that added up to me riding past miles of ranchland of cattle grazing undisturbed on a peaceful morning.

It is possible to ride a big motorcycle and cry at the same time. I know this because I did it that morning. It was a combination of the overwhelming beauty of the place and the realization I had lived to see yet another vista, another special place. I had persevered through all the suffering and uncertainty of cancer and had gotten to this place, this wonderful, beautiful, spectacular piece of God's wonderful creation and had paid the cancer price of admission to get there. I was so very, very grateful to have made it there to a place I had never heard of which had been spared and left for me to gaze upon and keep as a cherished memory of healing and restoration.

I pray a lot. It kind of goes with the territory of being a holy man. People more or less expect praying to be something a minister does. A lot of that sort of prayer is professional, public prayer, delivered in a church worship setting. It is usually constrained by the liturgical preferences of the congregation. It is part of the job to do it and can be a very spiritual thing. It can also just be another rote exercise in getting through the service. My prayers in the Gypsum Hills were of a different kind entirely that morning. No flowery sentences, no politically correct construct. Just words of joy and profound appreciation to God who had seen me through my nightmare. I had walked through the valley of the shadow of death and he had been there with me. Riding in the Gypsum Hills that morning was my moment of stepping out of the valley of the shadow and walking back into the land of the living and I was so happy to have made it through. Who cares about bedbugs or fleas or Styrofoam coffee cups when you can embrace the moment of your awareness of continuing life in a place as spectacular as this? I was alive and moving forward on a path of my choosing. I had made it.

***　　　***　　　***　　　***　　　***

I was having a good time rolling through the Gypsum Hills and I hoped it would be an all-day thing. That illusion was shattered after a few hours when I left the hills and rode onto the flat plains of western Kansas. I was back in wind turbine country again and this time it was large, much larger than the day before. I have had some scary times on my bike. Those usually involved wet roads or inattentive drivers. Those things turned out to be nothing compared to trying to pilot my bike through these terrifying crosswinds. I was wearing my adventure helmet which has a substantial black plastic visor attached. It serves as a kind of sunshade, or cap bill if you will, and I had grown to like the little extra defense against the sun it provided me. Unfortunately, it also proved to be a sail in the wind when it was grabbed by the crosswinds. I have no idea how fast the wind was blowing. What I do know is it was strong enough to throw me to the side of my bike and yank my bike into opposing lanes of traffic without any warning. At one point during one of these terrifying wind blast episodes I had been blown into the opposite lane of travel and tractor trailer rigs were coming at me head-on. This happened more than once that day and each time I would see the oncoming tractor trailers—sometimes pulling just one trailer and other times two or more—start a crazy serpentine wiggle as the wind pulled and pushed them across the yellow center line. We were all fighting for survival out there and if I had given any thought to the potential disaster that could unfold I would have stopped until the wind died down. As it was, I just leaned as hard as I could on my handlebars and pushed my body against the wind and somehow we all missed each other. On one particularly straight stretch, I was in a line behind two other motorcycles I had come upon as I rode. They were Harley cruisers and those guys were fighting as hard as I was to stay on our side of the road. We were all three dangerously losing the battle, so much so that the oncoming traffic pulled off their side of the road and waited for us to fight it out and pass them. I concluded that this sort of thing happened all the time out there and motorists have developed the sensible manners of pulling over and letting the idiots on the bikes duke it out with Mother Nature as best they can. At any rate, I was very happy to see two clear lanes for our use.

After two hours of this I was worn out, so I began looking for a place to eat. I was not inclined to be real picky. If I could find a restaurant and it had a parking lot I could get my bike into, then I was going to stop and eat whatever they had on the menu. I found a little Mexican restaurant situated in a simple, one-story, red brick building residing in the middle of a gravel parking lot on the side of the road just north of the Kansas/Texas border. I don't know the name of the place, but I do remember the "For Sale" sign was larger than the business sign. The parking lot had one car and one truck in it when I pulled in. I shed my helmet and gloves and walked through the door to discover I was the only Anglo in the place. There were three Hispanic folks sitting at two tables. One was an elderly gentleman. There was a handsome woman in her 40s who seemed to run the place and finally a young teenager who turned out to be my waiter. I sat at a table and looked around. It soon became apparent this was a family-owned operation and the elderly gentleman was the grandfather. When the teenager was not quick enough in bringing me a menu, the grandfather called out to the mother who called out to the teenager whom I presumed to be her son and the menu got delivered without further delay. Everyone in there was pleasant and the place was clean. I found that I was starving after the rough ride I had just made so I ordered a deluxe combo plate. When the boy asked me what I wanted to drink, I ordered a diet drink. He came back in a few minutes and told me they were out of diet, so I ordered another drink. I think it was a 7Up. He came back in a few minutes and told me they were out of that too. I then told him I would have whatever they had available. He replied that was good because all they had was Dr. Pepper. So, I lost five minutes of my life ordering Dr. Pepper. That's how it goes with teenagers.

The food was really good, which proves a point I was to learn over and over again on the road: Some of the very best meals are to be had in places that look like you should pass them by. I think the armor I wore under my coat alarmed the owners until they saw me remove it and set it on one of the chairs at my table. Maybe it looked like I was wearing combat gear or I was some sort of government officer. Whatever it was, when I took the gear off and they saw I was wearing ordinary clothes underneath, they relaxed.

I finished my meal while studying travel times using my iPad maps. I would be at Eagle Nest, New Mexico before dark if I made good time. The roads through this corner of Kansas, Texas and Oklahoma had some twists and turns, but I felt I could make it. I made some notes on an index card and stuck it in my tank bag window to use for a glancing point of reference as I rode. One of the things I decided before my trip was to keep the noise out of my helmet and I did so to the point of not having navigation speakers inside the helmet and wearing ear plugs every day. This old-fashioned decision forced me to really study my maps and be aware of road signs and the position of the sun at all times. I was going to cross the continent like explorers had done it for centuries—using a map and the sun. The computer was on my bike, but I would get myself to my destination.

I made a few wrong turns in that tristate area owing mostly to me not trusting my sense of direction and recollection of my maps. At one point, I rode 15 miles in the wrong direction going north when I should have been going southwest. I finally decided to trust my initial reading of things and I turned around and was soon back on track. This particular folly resulted in me riding through the wind turbine gauntlet for an extra 15 miles, but it was the worst mistake I made on the trip.

I was excited about reaching New Mexico. I was on only day three of the ride and I would be there before dark. The longer I rode, the more excited I became. I knew it was in my best interest to get off the bike and calm down before I made a mistake and wrecked, so I pulled over at the first historical marker and walked around for a while. The break from riding had its desired effect and my excitement ebbed to manageable proportions. I got back on and soon crossed the border into New Mexico. I was in the northeastern part of the state with my destination being the little town of Eagle Nest. It's a small resort community of about 375 people sitting at an elevation of 8,240 feet in the Sangre De Cristo Mountains. The air is high country clean and cool for most of the year. The village is nestled on the shores of Eagle Nest Lake. It's a place where people go to camp, fish, ski and just generally relax in a rural alpine setting devoid of the commercialism of a huge ski resort community. Think *Northern Exposure* if you are of an age that television show resonates and you have the idea. There was supposed to be a campground nearby and it was my hope to throw up my tent for the night and check out the Laguna Vista Bar which was being touted in magazine advertisements as "The Best Bar in the West." More on that a little bit later.

Before there could be Eagle Nest, before there could be the Laguna Vista Bar, before there was a tent and sleep, I had to get there. Within just a few miles of getting on the New Mexico backroads, I knew I was in for a treat. The land was stunning ranchland boasting undeveloped vistas for miles and miles. The character of the roads was a bikers dream—curvy and twisting, but no pothole ridden switchbacks or blind curves. Just miles and miles of undulating and winding road set in the midst of gorgeous valleys surrounded by mountains that were alternately catching the rays of the sun and then throwing off gigantic shadows that went for miles. As I rode I could see a large thunderstorm complete with heavy lightning bouncing off the mountains. It was no small storm. I kept trying to locate the storm as I rode and it kept moving as the road kept twisting. All I knew was wherever that thing was, the people underneath were going to get the crap kicked out of them.

While I wasn't seeing many cars up to this point, I did encounter greeters along the way in the form of occasional herds of antelope. They are really North American pronghorns, but most folks refer to them as antelope. I love the little fellas. I have hunted them over the years, but I am just as content to watch them graze and walk along the prairie. The North American pronghorn is a prehistoric connection to this continent as it emerged from the Ice Age. You will find the pronghorn represented in a lot of prehistoric artwork. As a species, it is a true survivor using a combination of extraordinary eyesight and speed to remain long after more impressive animals like the wooly mammoth have passed from the stage. Unlike deer, they do not have a death wish and do not run out in front of cars and motorcycles at every opportunity. They are curious little guys who like to look you up and down as you ride by. I passed two antelopes who were no more than five feet from me and they were perfectly content to just stand there and watch the big yellow banana man ride on by on his motorcycle.

I was keeping an eye on the storm as I made my way through the mountain valleys and passes. It soon became apparent I was going to be one of the unfortunate souls who was going to be underneath the storm. I was in such a remote area there were no gas stations, houses or barns. Just fence, cattle and antelopes. I was in real danger now. Lightning was really lighting up the skies and bouncing off every high point I could see. Contrary to the layman's assumption, motorcyclists can be struck by lightning. Most people think it is the tires that insulate a motorist from the dangers of a lightning strike. In reality, it is the metal cage of the car that protect the motorist inside since the metal acts as a lightning rod to guide the electricity around the passengers. There is no metal to surround a motorcyclist, so we are the high point on the bike and very vulnerable.

By now several cars were behind me and the rain was coming down in buckets. I switched my bike's ride computer over to the "Rain" setting which instantly improved the traction and handling. The road was covered in pools of water and there was no place to pull off. I came around a curve and saw the road completely submerged in a large pool of water. Both lanes were blocked and I could not see the painted lines so I knew there were several inches of water on the road. My speed was around 55 mph since I was being pushed by the cars behind me. I had no choice except to hit the puddle and hope for the best. Applying my brakes would have resulted in being run over from behind by the car which was for all practical purposes tailgating me.

I love the German engineers. The rain setting, which is a computer setting that senses decreased friction and slippage on the tires caused by water and then compensates to keep the bike upright and in contact with the road surface, worked perfectly and kept my bike stable and on course. I like to think I did a fair amount of really good riding at that moment because I did not panic and I resisted the temptation to fight the bike. I was through the puddle in just a second and then it was onto the next curve and the next bolt of lightning. The storm had spent itself within the hour and was gone as quickly as it came. I was back on dry road and the sun was shining.

It was also getting a lot, lot cooler as I climbed in elevation. I began to wonder if I would need to stop and put on more clothes, but I decided I could make it and kept on going. Eagle Nest would be just up the road and I sure wanted to get my money's worth out of the remaining daylight and this beautiful country.

I look back on those few hours in the rain and have to admit that while it was a scary time, it was also exhilarating and life-infusing. I am not a thrill seeker or an adrenaline junkie by any means. At the same time, there is a certain social contract the rider has to enter into with the sport to accept the risks inherent in the undertaking. Motorcycling is not as safe as knitting, but it is certainly a great way to travel, see the world and learn a great deal about oneself in the process. The key for me in motorcycling, as it has always been in my big game hunting, is careful planning and training so that I am minimizing the risks that are out there.

Planning is more than spending a bunch of money on equipment, although you absolutely need the right gear for the job. Planning means physical training to ensure your fitness for the sport. I spent far more time riding my bicycle getting ready for this ride than I did on the motorcycle. I wanted my legs and stamina to be fit so I could manage the physicality of long riding. Those days in the wind and rain, while not made insignificant by my training, were certainly much more manageable because I was in shape for the trip. Yes, I had good gear, but I also made sure my 57-year-old body was ready for the task at hand as well. Good planning is also a daily thing when a solo rider is out on the road. I made sure I got plenty of rest each night and I kept alcohol consumption to a minimum. Alcohol is relaxing at night, but you pay for it the next morning on the bike. I stayed hydrated during the day drinking water constantly out of my CamelBak and I ate light while I rode so I would not get sleepy.

The mental aspect of riding is perhaps its greatest joy and

also its greatest risk. The sensory overload a rider can experience is a true natural high and leads to terrific lifelong memories. Let the body get tired and dehydrated and spend too long in the saddle and then the brain becomes a dangerous instrument. Reflexes begin to fail, judgment is impaired and knowing left from right can become difficult if not impossible. When the rider senses those things starting to happen, the ride is over no matter where the rider finds himself at that moment. You just park the bike and rest and live to ride another day. I was fortunate on the trip to have that happen only once and it was much later in the ride. My approach to Eagle Nest found me to be tired, but so excited over spending my first night in New Mexico that I could have ridden for many more hours had I felt the need. I saw signs up ahead for Eagle Nest and I turned my attention to finding the campground.

***   ***   ***   ***   ***

I don't know why camping was such a problem on this trip. I was sure that no matter where I went there would be empty campsites everywhere. Not so at Eagle Nest. The campground was completely full of fisherman and a sizeable contingent of Rainbow people who were just lying down and sleeping where the mood and the ganja struck them. So, it was back to finding a room for the night.

I knew I was going to the Laguna Vista Bar and I knew there was a hotel by the same name, so I tried my luck and hit pay dirt. The owner was the desk clerk and he was a biker who wanted to help out a brother so he put me up in a really nice sea blue room with a swordfish seashell motif. The room was super clean with nice furniture in a Florida wicker condo sort of way and there were plenty of towels. The world famous bar was in the building next door so I was good to go.

I hit the shower and let the price-included hot water warm my rain-chilled bones. A shower is something we take for granted on a day-in, day-out basis, but spend hours in cold mountain rain and the hot water coursing down your head and onto your aching shoulders is a pretty good deal. I let the hot water turn me into a high mountain red version of a six-foot-one lobster before I got out.

By now it was time for me to wash some clothes since I had brought only three days' worth of everything. I figured it would be all I needed since the advertisements said all of this gear would practically be dry as soon as you wrung it out after a hand washing. Did I mention that advertising people are lying bastards? Did I mention that underwear doesn't dry out instantly after it's wrung out? Did I mention that advertising people are lying bastards?

I hung up my still very wet underwear and socks and walked over to the world famous Laguna Vista Bar. Did I mention that advertising people are lying bastards? The bar was, well, just an ordinary, very ordinary restaurant bar with cheap, two-quarters pool tables. Bars in bowling alleys are infinitely better and more fun. The place was dead as a doornail and there was no beer on tap. If you wanted a beer, the old bartender grabbed one out of a refrigerator and opened it with a bottle opener. He was wearing a tie and he called me sir, but that was about it. To make matters worse, the bar had no Makers Mark. You can't, in this Kentuckian's opinion, be a world famous bar if you don't have Maker's Mark. I stayed for a few minutes scoping the place out without ordering a bottled beer. I had little airline size bottles of Maker's Mark in my room and preferred my own company and some map study to that of a pop top bartender. One plus of staying at the hotel which owned the bar was getting a free bag of ice from the pop top bartender. It's not often a bartender in a bow tie will give a patron a carryout bag of ice, so I suppose that counts for something. I took my bag of ice and got the hell out of there and went back to my room. I was tired anyway and my Maker's Mark was calling.

I decided to go for a walk before I returned to my room for the night, so I dropped the bag of ice off in the room (my instant dry underwear and socks were still wet) and went for a walk toward the campground and lake which was just outside of town. I stopped in at the local gas station to get some chips to go with my Kentucky bourbon and was greeted by a nice Native American cashier. She could tell I was from out of town and the usual conversation ensued about my origins and destinations. I got around to asking her why the bar was absolutely dead at 8:30 in the evening. She told me the next day was the annual "Fish For Free" day in New Mexico when you could fish without a license and that everyone in town was gearing up for the big day. I asked her what kind of fish everyone would be after and she told me "bluegill."

There you have it. If you want your man to give up the bottle.

If you want your best friend to take the pledge and swear off the demon rum. Just get them to take up bluegill fishing. At least in New Mexico. I can say for certain it would be a failure in Kentucky since any true Kentuckian knows how to drink and fish at the same time, but to each his own.

I returned to my room with an excellent bag of Cheetos and enjoyed Maker's Mark with Diet 7Up. The gas station people were better stocked than the "All we have is Dr. Pepper" Mexican restaurant. I had ridden 475 miles on day three and I was tired, having fought wind and rain for hours. I was going to ride less tomorrow. My plan was to ride to Santa Fe and get the bike's computers run through a diagnostic to determine why the false codes were coming up on the instrument panel. I would take it easy getting there and then decide where to go after I left the Santa Fe BMW dealer.

Before turning in, I checked my underwear one more time. They were still soaked. It was obvious I was going to ride in wet underwear the next day if I did not come up with a solution. So, I did what all great adventurers do when faced with similar circumstances. I grabbed the hotel-provided hair dryer and turned it into an underwear dryer by blowing hot air inch-by-snail's-pace-inch over each garment until they were dry. I think I blew the dryer up because it began to groan and blow cold air after the first 30 minutes. By then, I had some dry garments so the project had been a success. My plan was to be on the road for 17 days. With only three days of clothes packed, I was not looking forward to the days when I would be camping with no hair dryer at the ready.

The road is a great teacher. Bars aren't always as advertised and gear doesn't always perform as stated. On the other hand, little out-of-the-way restaurants cook some great food and German engineers know a lot about building bikes to ride in thunderstorms. Some people like to fish for free and a biker brother makes a nice room available for a tired rider.

I was having fun now. The road was coming alive and I had reached New Mexico.

The chrysalis was out of its cocoon and wings were spreading.

Pictures from the Road

Here is my rock solid GS on the day we came together:

Here is how the V-Strom looked the day I left on my first overnight camping adventure to Columbus-Belmont State Park on the shores of the Mississippi River in far Western Kentucky:

Here is the War Room:

Here is a close-up of the map as it looked toward the end of my route-planning:

All loaded up and ready to go the night before departure:

Here we are on June 3, 2015, the day we left to ride to New Mexico on my "I'm Still Here Tour 2015" ride:

On the way to Silver City:

The Brits at the Toad:

The lobby of the Murray Hotel:

Nick Sanders' motorcycle:

A pretty pastoral scene of the barn across the road from the Honeysuckle Inn in Missouri:

Just after I rode across the border into New Mexico:

This is the burger drive-in in Caney, Kansas where I met Big Ed and the crazy cowboy:

This is the mondo green chili burrito I had for breakfast that morning in Eagle Nest when I learned about "T-Plus love":

I stopped at the Corvette Museum in Bowling Green on my way west:

Beer and fried pickles—my dinner that night in Missouri at the sports bar that wasn't really a sports bar:

Parked in front of the old Merit Suit factory, Mayfield, KY:

Eagle Nest, NM with my bike in the hotel parking lot:

Wearing a minister's hat with my bike:

Riding up into the Sacramento Mountains to Cloudcroft, NM:

My meager Vienna sausage and donated crackers dinner on my first night on the road home somewhere in Texas:

My burger and milkshake meal at Belew's in Kentucky Lake country on the return trip home:

Riding through the White Sands Missile range on the way to Alamogordo:

A cockpit view of the road on my way to Alamogordo:

A pair of sunsets in Alamogordo, New Mexico

Chapter 10

Day Four

All Kinds of People

-----Original Message-----
From: Brian House
Sent: Sunday, June 07, 2015 12:48 AM

Today was a day of meeting people. I rode 325 miles from Eagle Nest through Taos then onto Santa Fe before heading south to Alamogordo. The ride was great, but it all started with people.

When I'm out on the road, I look for unusual places to eat. I'll hit the chains as a last resort, but if I have the opportunity I go for something less reliable and make it an adventure. I had a few choices for breakfast in Eagle Nest this morning. One was a big box affair that had a large sign emblazoned with the words "Country Kitchen." There were several cars parked in front of the establishment and most were rentals. Across the street was a little blue building, maybe 30 feet by 40. It was constructed of cinder block. At some point many years ago it had been painted a light blue. Now it was just a tired paler shade of its former self. A small sign hung above the door: "D&D Cafe." There were three pickup trucks parked outside. It had been years since any of them had been new on the showroom floor. I walked in and was greeted by the smell of freshly brewed coffee and bacon on the griddle. Things were looking up.

The "D&D" had only five tables in the whole place. The first table by the entrance was the "Liars Table" and it was occupied by the usual gathering of old men who assemble in places like this all over *the world every morning to share fellowship and generally let the world know they are not dead yet. I get that sort of thing now after my cancer journey. Anyway, one table was vacant at the back so I walked over and sat down. The old guys had the first two tables, then a loner was in the third and finally a couple was in the fourth. The old guys had it together in a cantankerous sort of way. Tables three and four were not in our solar system. Here is a little of what I heard while I was having my coffee:*

The lady (I named her "Mary" to protect her privacy) at Table Four talking to her male companion: "Awww, Sam ain't gonna be able to knock him down. He's got that T-plus love."

I'll let you know when I figure out what "T-plus love" is.

The lead old guy at Table One was, at the same time, in the midst of explaining to his crowd how his brother, who couldn't serve in the Korean War because he "knocked up" his wife, is doing now health-wise. He is doing better now that "they have changed his medication."

Back to Mary at Table Four: "I think my neighbor thinks he's a dog. He kind of looks like one the way he lays down in the yard."

Back to the old guys at Table One, who pretty much explained to everyone in the D&D how to mow a yard and service a riding mower. All of them apparently were expert yard mowers. Then the head old guy at Table One yells at the cook, "I'd like my breakfast before dinner tonight!" to which the cook told him to shut up or he would get his breakfast on a stick.

Then the guy at Table Three caught my attention. Actually, I noticed him before I even listened to the others. It was hard to miss him since he had been smiling at everyone and talking to the wall and the baseball card collection that is framed and hung on the wall facing his table. He gets ready to leave and walks over to me and tells me he is a diamond cutter who works at a secret diamond cutting location on his uncle's ranch outside of Eagle Nest. He says it's not his real job, but he'll keep doing it for the next five years "until the investigation is over and things die down." Says he was a pilot about 40 years ago and has been to the airport to rent a plane and is sure it "will all come back to him as soon as he is in the air."

Back to Table One, the head old guy yelling at the cook again who still hasn't fixed his breakfast: "Well, if you can't cook, some coffee would be nice."

And all of this before I had ridden one mile.

This is what makes solo travel so very special. Out on the road, unencumbered by the proprieties of companionship, a lone rider is free to embrace the world on its terms. People see us and ask us questions and on some very rare occasions, like this morning at the D&D, we are welcomed into the ordinary lives of folks we will never see again. That one hour at the D&D made the entire trip for me. Fortunately, the ride continues.

I left the D&D wondering why I had ordered the giant double fiery green chili breakfast burrito along with four cups of coffee. Blame it on the entertainment. After a short walk back to the motel, I loaded the bike and hit the ignition. That's when the little Bavarian engineers interfered with my trip. The day before it had been the check oil light and the engine temperature warning. This morning the ASC (Stability Control) and the ABS (Antilock brakes) alerts were blinking at me. I pulled out the manual and cleared the ASC, but the ABS would not resolve. There was nothing for it but to go to the BMW dealer in Santa Fe. I planned a route through half of the enchanted circle of the Taos ride and went at it. If the ABS wasn't working, then it didn't matter because the GS took the countless curves and turns with no problem. Fortunately, the little BMW GPS has all BMW dealers' addresses in America preloaded in the computer. With a punch of a button my route was programmed into the screen of the GPS and I was off on a guided route to the dealership.

The Santa Fe dealer shares space with the BMW automobile dealer, which translates into some really nice real estate. A young man named Tao greeted me at the door. I explained my problem with the fault indicators. He immediately took the GS back to the technician who ran a diagnostic on the bike. In short order, he told me there was nothing wrong with it. It's just those German computers. He said the BMW computers are very sensitive. Well, I'm sensitive too, but I didn't say anything. It does occur to me that BMW needs to get their obsessive German engineers to tone it down a little on the sensitivity of their stuff. I'm all for knowing what wizards those guys are, but I really didn't relish driving through downtown Santa Fe on a Saturday when everybody and their mother was trying to get out of town. Still, it must be noted how very professional and prompt the Santa Fe dealer's staff was to me. While the bike was being checked out, Tao gave me a tour of the facility and showed me the new bikes as well as a customized Iron Butt GS that looked more complicated than a spaceship. All in all, I had a good time there.

I decided to head south to Alamogordo. Now, you won't find that town on any list of great rides. Alamogordo matters to me because that is where USAF First Lieutenant Elliott House will be spending the next three years of his life defending his country. Lt. House is my son and I decided to exercise the "Focker Prerogative" and go check things out firsthand to make sure the Air Force would meet my expectations.

The ride was unremarkable until I was clear of Albuquerque. I took a few side roads through Indian reservations, but it was I-25 until Highway 380, which was stunning in its desert beauty. As I was riding along 380, I realized there were no buildings of any kind. Nothing. Not one. Hadn't been for miles. It occurred to me someone could make a killing developing this beautiful place. According to my GPS, there were plenty of streets in this area and all of them had the same initials followed by different numbers: "WSMR". Hmmm... and then I saw the big sign. Wait for it. "White Sands Missile Range." I was riding through the place where our government teaches its aspiring missile shooters how to shoot missiles and bombs and assorted instruments of destruction. The German Luftwaffe has resident pilots at Holloman AFB learning how to fly and shoot stuff from the platform of our new Raptor fighter jets. So, basically I was riding through a target. Comforting.

I'm going to hang around Alamogordo for a few days and learn some more about the place while taking a day ride tomorrow. Every day has been a blast. It's the unexpected that makes it so much fun. I think life is like that too. We can all get by doing the predictable and the very planned out, but it's how we adapt and manage the unforeseen and difficult that define who we are in the end.

I'm looking forward to another interesting breakfast tomorrow.

Be safe,
Brian

***　　　***　　　***　　　***　　　***

The late, great Gonzo journalist Hunter S. Thompson once wrote, "When the going gets weird, the weird turn pro." Well, I have no doubt that I met the By God Starting Line-up of the Weird of the Universe's All Star Team at the D&D Restaurant that morning in Eagle Nest. The conversations that were taking place around me were so unhinged, so detached from reality that I will go to my grave never knowing whether these people and their bizarre conversations were real or whether my hippie waiter slipped acid into my mondo burrito and sent me on the LSD trip of a lifetime.

I could have avoided all of these delightfully interesting people by just taking the safe play and going to the tourist trap buffet across the road, but then that would have meant things like "T-Plus love" and "I'm sure I'll get the hang of flying once I'm back in the air" would not be part of my memory. Strange as that breakfast was, it now occupies an almost black light glowing spot on the canvas of my memory of the trip.

It's not so much that these people said these things, and say them they did because I was writing their conversations down as fast as I could while I sat at my table at the D&D so I would not lose a single phrase. It was that in hearing it all I rightly asked myself the question, "What made these people who they are?" You can't go to school and take classes to turn out like that.

Ms. T-Plus Love "Mary" was a well-worn blonde in her late 30s and was already gaining the weight that would remind her that she was no longer a girl. Her eyes were tired and her skin had the pallor of someone who spends too much time indoors drinking coffee and smoking cigarettes. Her breakfast companion was a man who wore his hair in a single braid that went to his waist. He sported a black cowboy hat adorned with silver Conchos and a blue feather. He appeared to be at least part Indian. He was very kind and attentive to her and understood the zone of her conversation. He obviously knew the parties mentioned in the conversation and was content to just nod his head and offer in only an occasional word. I don't blame him. I would play it safe and let the T-Plus love just wash all over me.

They were the first people to finish their meal and leave. As they got up she looked at me and smiled in a tired almost apologetic sort of way, as if to say, "I am who I am. I hope I didn't bother you." They left and walked out the door out of my view down the street. I noticed she had left her purse on the floor by her chair, so I picked it up and took it to my very funny and much-tattooed waiter, who was also doing double duty as a cashier. He was very thin, of indeterminate middle age and wore cut-off jeans with low top Chuck Taylors giving him traction. I told him she had forgotten her purse. One of the old guys at Table One heard me and he said out loud to everyone in the place:

"That's 'Mary.' (The named is changed to protect the innocent.) She does stuff like that all the time."

"Mary" came back in toward the end of my meal and asked for her purse. My waiter turned cashier was polite and soft-spoken with her. It was obvious everyone in the D&D knew her and shared the knowledge of her unspoken history. There would be no judging her in the D&D. Maybe in a main street church of uptown Baptists, but not here. The cashier must have told her I found her purse because she looked at me with tears in her eyes and said, "Stuff like this happens to me all the time." And then she was out the door wiping tears away as she went. I never saw her again.

The loner who told me he was a diamond cutter on the lam I dubbed Mr. Witness Protection (WP for short). He was not playing with a full deck by any means, but he was sure as hell great breakfast entertainment. He was in his 60s and was someone who had no trouble carrying on a conversation since he didn't discriminate between animate and inanimate objects when it came to speaking and listening. Just who he thought he was and who he thought he saw when he was up and about is a mystery. What amazed me was WP's obvious intelligence. This was not an uneducated man, yet there had been a short-circuiting of his system and he was no longer fully there. The old guys at the liars table, the waiter and the fry cook owner all knew him. He was a regular and posed no threat to anyone in the place. He was welcome to come and go at the D&D for as long as he wanted, and for that matter so was I. People were friendly to me and asked me what I came to call the "Road Questions"— where was I from and where was I going. When I told them Kentucky to Alamogordo on a motorcycle, a few of the old guys began to regale me with stories of their motorcycle days. None of them could believe I had traveled so far alone and yet I knew some of them had no doubt traveled to the jungles of the Pacific War campaign and the forests of Europe to fight Hitler and had never considered that out of the ordinary.

I hated for that breakfast to end. Those folks were the best therapy I'd had in months. Watching them make it through the confusing and painful clutter that made up their lives reminded me we all get nicked and battered and just have to do our best to carry on. We may walk a little slower or invent something called "T-Plus Love" just to give the face in the mirror a little hope to start the day, but we get through the day and make it one way or the other.

I left the good food and great people behind and started out to Santa Fe. I took a route toward Taos on a road called "The Enchanted Highway" that would eventually put me in the general direction of Santa Fe. The road took me through alpine forests winding alongside brilliantly clear, fast-moving mountain streams. I kept a leisurely pace and enjoyed the terrific balance of the bike as I leaned from one side to the other through the many curves. I reached Santa Fe in a few hours all the while wishing the ride had lasted longer and made my way to the BMW dealer. I would never have found the place had I not had the GPS to guide me.

It was nice to deal with people who wanted to help me for a change. While my bike was getting the once over, I talked to an Iron Butt rider. He was a surgeon from back east who was doing a series of 1,000-mile days back to back. Yes, that's right, "thousand-mile days." To be an Iron Butt rider, you have to ride an approved route following some pretty strict rules designed to keep you alive and prevent cheating and ride 1,000 miles in 24 hours. It is a hard thing to do and poses all the risks you would think are inherent in riding anything that far in that short amount of time. Add to the distance factor the simple problems of time and sitting, the risks of wind, weather, deer and road debris and you begin to get the idea that Iron Butt riders are a special breed and they are.

The Iron Butt rider had no ego and was not interested in trying to impress me. He answered the few questions my inexperienced rider's mind could muster up to ask him and then he was off to drink bottled water and take a nap while his bike was serviced.

My bike was declared fit for service in less than an hour and I was on my way. It took a while to ride through the bumper-to-bumper traffic of people wanting to get out of town to the mountains for the weekend, but I eventually made it. I always had my most difficult time navigating in the cities. This is when the Bluetooth communication for my navigation computer would have made it much easier, but I wanted to do it by looking at the maps and deciding where to go.

Once I was out of town, I stopped and gave my maps another look and realized I would need to be on the interstate for a while since there were no clearly marked roads to get me through to the Alamogordo area. I'm sure they were there, but this was an area I had not studied since I never envisioned my brand new bike needing a shop call this early in the trip. So interstates it was.

Some riders don't mind interstates. Some of the riders who ride the really big bikes like the Honda Goldwing or biggest Harleys will spend days on the interstate and think nothing of it because their bikes handle the wind and truck blasts so much better. My bike is in the 500-pound category and can handle interstates just fine, but it can do so very much more on backroads than the big bikes if given a chance. I was determined to give it that chance as often as I could. I kept my interstate time to the bare minimum and only rode them when I had no other choice. The speeds are too great and you just can't see a community or have a chance to meet people if all you are doing is riding from one interstate gas station to another. I was making much slower time, but I was seeing what I wanted to see.

I eventually exited the interstate and got onto Highway 380 headed south. This road was beautiful. Some stretches of it were straight to and beyond the horizon. The road was also more or less deserted. I reveled in the solitude, the sheer absence of humanity; the kinds of things that are hard to find when you are riding a bike east of the Mississippi where there are so many more people and communities per square mile.

I rode for quite a while through the White Sands Missile Range. The range is hundreds of square miles of open and generally flat country and is used by our military to train jet and drone pilots and the teams that make up missile batteries. It is ideal for pilots to make bombing runs and for drone pilots to practice their skills. I turned down a few side roads and took some pictures for my trip and used the time off the bike to rest on the side of the road.

It struck me that what was going on here within the confines of that massive range was the training of human beings to exercise their skills, demonstrating the greatest precision with their equipment to someday destroy my country's enemies. These young men and women were learning a skill that would destroy the lives and property of some other country in order to save the lives and way of life of others including me. I realized they were much like my oncology team. My cancer doctors are trained to kill the thing that had tried to kill me and so many others. Their bombs are radiation rays and their jets are the robots they use to kill the cancer living inside their patients. Theirs is a battlefield of limited size, yet possessing all the gravitas and misery of Gettysburg or the Battle of the Bulge. Sometimes killing is a good thing. I rode out of the White Sands Missile Range thankful for both the pilots and the doctors and their intentionally destructive life-saving skills.

It was at this point that my brain woke up and I realized that with the day winding down fast and I still about 60 miles from Alamogordo, I did not have a place to stay that night. Prior to leaving on my trip, I had worked things out so Susan, my son and his new bride could spend a long week in Florida. Now, while I was a big sweating banana standing in the middle of a bomb and missile target in New Mexico, they were lounging comfortably on the beach sipping drinks and soaking up rays. I interrupted Susan's revelry and called her and asked for her help in finding me a room. She is the master and gatekeeper of all our hotel points and the programs we use to accumulate them. I did not want to commit the cardinal sin of staying somewhere and not getting points when I could have stayed across the street and earned those precious things. So, I called and asked for her help. By the time I reached Alamogordo, a text was buzzing on my phone to let me know she had found a hotel with a points earning room. All was good.

It was time to get to the hotel and unpack, stow away and clean up before dinner. Fortunately, the Hampton Inn where I was staying has a new Applebee's right next door, so I was able to walk into their sports bar and have a meal while watching baseball on three screens. A salad and an ice cold beer and all was good.

I had started the day with people who floated well out of reality, met a guy with an Iron Butt, rode through alpine meadows and stopped to take pictures in a missile range.

Without a doubt I had seen the "weird turn pro" and it was alright with me. We are all doing our best to be survivors. No doubt some of us do it with less stress than others, but in the end we all make it work out one way or the other.

It was time for another beer.

By the way, what in the world is "T-Plus love?"

Chapter 11

Day Five

What We Leave Behind

-----Original Message-----

From: Brian House
Sent: Sunday, June 07, 2015 11:12 PM

My ride today had me thinking about soap commercials from my childhood. There was one which used a "Springtime in the Mountains" theme. I think it was Irish Spring, but I'm not sure. Whatever it was, I sure had that same happy feeling on this ride.

I rode from Alamogordo up into the mountains east of there to the small town of Cloudcroft. It is a resort community that serves the various outdoor hobbies that take place in the Lincoln National Forest—skiing, snowboarding, camping, hiking and hunting, among others. The ride to Cloudcroft was a constant climb of turns and s-curves that made the 15-mile ride up a sheer delight.

I stopped for breakfast at one of the restaurants recommended by some search engine. The staff was clearly having a bad day with only one cook and waitress, but they were very pleasant people and a delight to talk to over a second cup of coffee. Somehow I never got a spoon to stir my coffee, but a little improvisation with a Splenda packet and all was fine.

I had it on my mind to buy a pair of those fancy hiking pants that have the zip off legs, and since there was a bike/hike shop just down the street I figured I was in luck. Who knew that you had to have either a 32 or 34-inch waist to be a hiker in New Mexico? I left with my unspent cash safely in my size 38 pants and went back to my bike.

I left Cloudcroft and rode a long loop through and around the forest over to the White Mountain Apache Reservation. Don't confuse this with the White Mountain Apache Reservation in eastern Arizona. Same tribe, different places. Cloudcroft is at about 8,750 feet elevation and the ride took me even higher. At one point the alpine forest thinned considerably and I thought I might ride above the timberline, but the road turned downward and back into the forest where I was greeted with more miles of wonderful curves and curves and curves. Most of you reading this know I am a novice at this type of riding. I kept wondering what a really experienced rider would have done on these roads. Still, I am confident I got my money's worth for the morning. I toured some National Forest campgrounds while I was up there and made plans to return and camp there tomorrow night. The campground host told me all of the Cloudcroft area campgrounds are pretty much full on the weekends but during the week you can have your pick. I'll let you know how my camping excursion went on my next post.

In the afternoon I wanted to visit two places in the area: White Sands National Monument and the Oliver Lee State Park. I made it to both of them.

White Sands National Monument abuts the White Sands Missile Range. The monument consists of thousands of acres of protected gypsum (I think) dunes. The dunes are formed by the effect of evaporation from nearby lakes. The residue is the gypsum which blows onto the dunes area as it has for millennia. Just imagine going to the beach without an ocean or water of any kind and you will understand the reality that is WSNM. There are picnic tables, grills, shelters, areas to play in the sand dunes and, instead of swimming, people sled down the dunes on the little round discs we all used to use on the snow when we were kids. The dunes are really tall so sledders pick up a lot of speed coming down the dunes. I watched several groups do this. It appeared the grandparents were content to sit under the sunshades and just watch, although they did seem to make frequent trips to their Yeti coolers to remove beverages and return to their beach chairs to drink them.

I used my nifty little BMW GPS to plan a route from WSNM to the

Oliver Lee State Park. Remember how I was complaining about the overly sensitive German engineers yesterday? Well, I take it back. I love them today. They have planned the GPS to configure routes based on available road surfaces. There was a perfectly safe and reliable route to the Oliver Lee on major highways, but the Germans would have none of it. Instead, they gave me backroads and gravel and red dirt and ruts and dips and, oh, I wish it had never ended. This GS is absolutely rock solid on those roads. Again I felt they were wasted on the likes of me, but I was glad to have taken my turn at it.

So why did I go to the Oliver Lee? If you're an Old West buff, you know who he was. If you're not, then I'll enlighten you. Oliver Lee and Albert Fountain were on opposite sides of the famous Lincoln County range wars of the late 1800s. Lee was ruthless in trying to become top dog in those parts. Fountain was a lawyer who wanted to stop what he perceived as Lee's land grab. Fountain ended up with a group of young men on his side who were known as the Regulators. They were all young men. One of those young fellows was William Bonney. You know him as Billy the Kid. Well, Lee hires Pat Garrett to kill the Kid which he did. Then someone ambushed Fountain and his eight-year-old son on the road. Their bodies were never found. Pat Garrett knew Lee hired it done and so Garrett went after Lee and had him brought to trial. Money talks and the money talked Lee into an acquittal. Later, Pat Garrett is ambushed and killed. Lee was the last man standing and he got it all. He got the land, he got the woman, he won elections and he was the founder of Alamogordo. He had many children and grandchildren. They still live here. They still have the same kind of clout old murdering Papaw Lee had, so they got a state park named after him. It's really a nice park with a well thought out campground and the restored Oliver Lee ranch house. When you visit, you owe it to your view of history to visit the place. It is a lasting reminder that the winner writes the history, no matter how many people he had to murder to be the winner.

I wrapped up my day with another, shorter backroads ride outside of Alamogordo having been to the mountaintop, the beach and then the home place of a really bad guy depending on how you read your history.

I'll ride some more backroads tomorrow and do some camping and let you know how it goes.

Be safe,
Brian

      ***   ***   ***   ***   ***

There is something about the vast mountainous forests and deserts of the American West that lends itself as a great place to do some thinking. The area around Alamogordo has way more than its share of vistas. There is the White Sands National Monument, which preserves this unusual area that is a beach without water. It is, at the same time, beautiful and deadly. The white dunes appear so soft and inviting, beckoning hikers and the curious ever deeper into the grasp of the dunes where the white gypsum reflects the sun with lethal vigor. People can die of thirst and exposure out there in a matter of a few hours and just a mile or so from their cars. Drive 20 miles down the road and up into the mountains and the temperature can be jacket weather on the same day people are dying in the dunes. The forests which surround Cloudcroft are vast, well-maintained and offer every kind of outdoor opportunity for those who like alpine sports, camping, hiking, mountain biking and even backroads for motorcycle riders like me. The seduction of the mountains is the sense that somehow by going higher in elevation, the individual is coming closer to whatever it is that makes the world go round. Moses encountered God in a burning bush on a mountain. Native Americans recognize many mountains as holy and sacred. The desert is equally capable of awakening the spiritual side of a person. Jesus walked into and out of the desert first to face his demons and overcome them, and then ultimately to begin his earthly ministry.

Life can be a desert, a place so bleak and unpromising that the one who suffers can seem lost and marooned in the desert of their life. When I was in seminary, we were taught that suffering people are often in the desert of their lives, and it is a very real and tangible experience for them. My pastoral counseling professor taught, "You don't go into the desert to drag the suffering person out. You go there to sit with them until they are ready to walk out on their own." That's a pretty cool little piece of wordsmithing and one several of us repeated when we would be sitting around drinking coffee after class. It sure made us sound pastoral, but then again, none of us had really had the chance to do the desert walk.

I entered my desert several years before this ride when my daughter was diagnosed with thyroid cancer. It was inconceivable to me that my child could be afflicted with cancer, but there it was. She had the disease and we had to deal with it. Surgery and radiation therapy and then more surgery followed. It was soul-crushing to go to bed and wake up every day with the knowledge my child was a cancer patient. Still, I made life go on and I continued working and pastoring churches and trying to have as normal a life as this sort of madness would permit.

There is a cadence to life, a steady step that it wants to take if we will just allow life to go forward. Life wants to carry on even when there are all kinds of terrible things happening to a family. It's how a species survives. People acknowledge the terrible, the unthinkable, the heart-breaking and then they grieve, cry out and curse God, ask forgiveness and then pick up what is left of life and carry on. This is how it went for my little family while we were going through the fresh hell of a child with cancer.

And then, just when we had time to breathe and think we were clear of cancer's terrible grasp, the worm turned again and I was diagnosed with prostate cancer. Life rewound back to the point of tests, scans, surgical decisions, no promises, then radiation, then no promises and then the living with the aftermath of tests and follow-up appointments that are every bit as nerve-racking as any call to run into battle has ever been. It never gets any easier. The cancer patient just gets to the point of functioning resignation, to where he can say, "The hell with it. I've done all I can do."

The life of my little family of four became a crucible of pain and fear and uncertainty. Still, we functioned. I practiced law and pastored churches while my daughter returned to work and my son continued onto graduate school. My wife carried all of our burdens and suffered as she loved us through it all, hoping and praying Sarah and I would somehow survive. Cancer is the great teacher of mortality. Most people are deniers of their transient existence. Cancer grabs you by the throat and lets you know you will be leaving and maybe sooner than later.

Fighting cancer takes time and it is the time as much as anything else that wears the patient down. The human brain does not have an effective "ON/OFF" button, and it keeps running in overdrive on those days between appointments and while waiting on test results. It is simply maddening. It is also a lonely existence.

I realized during my phase of active treatment that most people, no matter how good or well-intentioned, just have no idea how to respond to the news that a friend or family member has cancer. I concluded there are many reasons for the indifference shown to the one who is afflicted. Some people just fear the disease and choose to run from anyone who has cancer. Others have agendas of entertainment and wealth accumulation and permit no time for the giving of themselves to be with the sick. Others just plain don't care. They will go on with their lives and if you die of cancer you really meant nothing to them. What hurts the cancer patient is the realization there are a lot of the "I don't care" people in their lives. It happened to me and became part of my big pause, the time when I stepped back from my former everyday existence, got on a motorcycle and looked at my life.

I entered the darkest part of the desert when I walked through the doors of Norton Hospital in Louisville, Kentucky to undergo surgery. The post-operative pathologies would tell me whether the cancer had spread to my lymph nodes and seminal vesicles. Cancer in the lymph nodes cannot be cured and its presence there makes for a grimmer prognosis. This uncertainty was heavy on my mind as I walked through the doors to Admissions to register for the morning surgery.

The church members and friends who were there that day for me were venturing into the desert with me and my family. They were willing to sit with us as our time in the desert began. They prayed with us and waited with my family while I was an unconscious participant in the battle on the operating room table. They made life more bearable that day for all of us.

The good news was the local confinement of the cancer. It had not spread to my bones, lymph nodes or seminal vesicles. There would be treatment to come in the form of radiation therapy, but I was early in the game and had a fighting chance to live a long life. We returned home and I took a few weeks off work to heal and gather my thoughts for life ahead.

I am fortunate to have a home with a patio and a walled prayer garden along with some acreage of woods and a small stream. I started my recovery by shuffling out onto the patio, then to the prayer garden and after a few days I walked around in the yard. It was a slow process, but one which worked and saw me gain strength and mobility every day. Those were days of quiet and solitude of no sounds except those made by my little dog, cat and Susan as she checked on me. The phone would ring occasionally with Susan serving as the screener for the calls. I spoke to a few people, but not many. The surgery had fatigued me and I needed time to recover.

The body heals quicker than the mind. I was up and back at work in two weeks, and for that I am very thankful. I am the kind of person who likes to be busy and because I have a really busy law practice I was able to hit my stride as soon as I walked through the door of my little mountain law office. The mind was another thing altogether.

I have been a lawyer since 1981. I went to a good law school and was trained by really good lawyers. I studied hard and I worked hard and, like a lot of lawyers, developed a specialty area of practice that allowed me to concentrate my skill set on an area that met my individual abilities. I became a mediator in 1992 and found that not only did I like serving as a neutral, as mediators are called in academic parlance, but I was also good enough at it that litigants wanted to hire me to do it all the time. That meant a lot of repetition and opportunity to develop my skill set. When anyone becomes really good at what they do, this fund of knowledge and ability becomes a reservoir upon which we can draw when other things are going on in our lives. A few professionals have the ability to separate themselves from their personal miseries and carry on with their job at hand. I was very fortunate to find out I was one of those people. I could go to work as a cancer patient and begin a mediation and I would not think about cancer again until it was over. I would not become a cancer patient until the day was over and then my mind would remind me that I was no longer one of the unafflicted. I was one of those guys who "had it."

You reach a crossroads with what I call your cancer brain. You can constantly dwell on the disease and all the bad shit it can do to you, or you can look at the good news the doctors have given you and actually lean on the faith component of your life to trust the God who made you and pick up the pieces and carry on. I chose to lean and pick up the pieces. It did not all happen in one day, but choose I did.

There is an ascendant component to my personal theology and I guess it is in large part of my upbringing as a Baptist child attending a very traditional main street Baptist church whose preachers weekly proclaimed a vertical view of the world. Live the right way and up you go. Live the bad way and down you go. One is nice and cool and the other is hot.

I was in a very good mood that first Alamogordo morning riding up to Cloudcroft and the Lincoln National Forest. The longer I ascended on those winding roads, the thinner and cooler the air became. The desert gave way to forests and vistas that would stretch for miles. I had ridden through some blistering hot days to get here and found this mountain air to be a welcome respite from the cauldron that was the trip out. Cloudcroft has a population of less than a thousand, but it is so busy with tourists and the daily hustle and bustle necessary to take care of them that it seems much larger. It is a service-based economy directed toward tourists like me, so finding a place to eat was not hard. I happily parked my motorcycle, stowed my yellow banana coat and helmet and began walking around town, which is to say I walked down the two streets that make up the community. The buildings are mostly wood with a few brick. Restaurants, gift shops and churches are in the main drag. There are smaller, more narrow backroads that are little more than alleys that take people to their cabins or condos. Most are within walking distance of the restaurants. The pace of Cloudcroft is easy and laidback. It is a great place to come and heal and walk out of the desert and that is exactly what I did.

Part of my spiritual formation revolved around studying the life and works of the Trappist monk Thomas Merton. I have stayed at the monastery in Gethsemane, Kentucky where he lived for most of his monastic life. Those have been days and nights of observing the discipline of silence and keeping the vigils of the monastery arising at all hours to read, pray and sing the Psalter in the sanctuary of Gethsemane. I have done it for very short periods of time. Some monks have done it for many decades. Merton was one of those. Before he died in 1968, Merton had written prolifically on spirituality and, in later years, world peace and the call to end all war. He possessed a deep, abiding love for all of creation and all of humanity. He drew no distinctions of color, ethnicity, class or sexuality. His embrace of all peoples came to him in an epiphanal moment while standing at the corner of Walnut and Fourth Street in Louisville, Kentucky on March 18, 1958. Merton writes of that day:

"In Louisville, at the corner of Fourth and Walnut, in the center of the shopping district, I was suddenly overwhelmed with the realization that I loved all those people, that they were mine and I theirs, that we could not be alien to one another even though we were total strangers...There is no way of telling people that they are all walking around shining like the sun."

Merton's "Fourth and Walnut" moment was the watershed event in his life when it came to his perspective of others and his view of ministry. Standing that morning on the sidewalks of Cloudcroft watching the people walking around, I was aware of these people, all of these people, strangers to me but not to God, for God had made them all. They were His and He loved them and because He called me to serve Him, I was called to love all of them without ever knowing them or making assessments of who they were or were not. Not only was I called to love them, but in that moment, standing outside a restaurant up in the mountains of New Mexico, I realized what cancer had not killed, could never kill or take away from me. I loved the people God had made and I loved them all and would keep on loving them until my time here was over.

I finished my breakfast, got back on my bike and rode through the national forest following roads that looked on a map like they would give me a good view of the area and they did. Open meadows, forested glens, streams and flowers, horses grazing and cattle standing around in high mountain meadows—it was all there. The houses were few and far between. I encountered only light traffic so I rode slowly with my helmet visor raised so I could smell the air. The scent of the pine trees and the occasional whiff of horse dung filled the air. It was a life-affirming ride. Here in this remote place, people were living and working and finding value in their routines and God was pleased. It was good to have made the trip up the mountain. I planned on returning to camp there in a few days.

***　　　***　　　***　　　***　　　***

I know that when I visit national monuments and state parks I will encounter heavy traffic and tourists who are in a hurry, a real hurry, and just want to get out for the one quick picture with their camera phone and then be on their way. There is nothing wrong with that except it makes life dangerous for motorcyclists. So, I was more than a little careful as I pulled into the very busy parking lot at the White Sands National Monument. People were zipping in and out. I parked and went inside and got directions on how to navigate through the dunes and then I was out the door and on my bike.

There really is no other place in the United States like White Sands. Our government has had the wisdom to designate the place a national monument so it will be protected from development. Access to the dunes is regulated by a series of roads that can give the illusion of driving on a snow-covered surface. These white roads blended perfectly into the sand dunes and really made it look like a winter scene from the Arctic. They posed a real problem for me as a motorcyclist since the white stuff was sand sitting on blacktop and it was as slick as a ribbon. I slipped and slid around until I learned how to throttle through the stuff and then it became downright fun as long as I kept it under the speed limit. There were rangers posted along the way watching our speeds. Apparently some other motorcyclists before me had figured out how to have fun out there. I rode the big loop around the park area and then headed my bike toward the Oliver Lee State Park. I used my GPS to plot a route over backroads to the park. Both the White Sands National Monument and the Oliver Lee State Park are located on the outskirts of Alamogordo. All of them are in the Tularosa Basin of the Chihuahuan desert. The Sacramento Mountains border the basin on the east and the White Sands are on the west. The Oliver Lee State Park is on the east. The Tularosa Basin is a closed basin, meaning no water flows out of it. Water flows down the mountains into the basin, but the evaporation leaves the water full of minerals and dissolved solids. Old timers called this type of water "brackish" which meant it was too salty too drink, which made life very hard in the basin. Irrigation was a big deal in pioneer times and those who understood how to engineer the movement of water did quite well for themselves. Oliver Lee was one of the men who knew men who could move water, and after some general lawlessness in the region, Lee came out on top. Depending on which version of history you believe, he was either a great visionary or an outlaw, but it makes no matter since old Oliver is dead and gone and the basin continues as it has for millennia.

There was a museum at the park that contained Oliver Lee's saddle, rifle and old tools and artifacts from the Old West. Me being the Old West buff that I am, I just had to pay the park a visit. The park visitors center was well-maintained and staffed by friendly people. I spent an hour or so there and then rode on. One of the hidden beauties of the West is the nature of the road system. In the East, even in southeastern Kentucky where I live, most of the roads are paved. Paving is necessary because of the harsh weather and the slope and grade of the roads. Leaving the roads in dirt or gravel and highway traffic would reduce them to impassable ruts after a few rains. The arid deserts of the southwest give highway engineers a lot more leeway when it comes to the surface selection. Main highways are all paved, but it is not at all unusual to find miles upon miles of unpaved road. Some is graveled, but a lot of it is just rich red hard packed dirt. This is a biker's delight and I reveled in it on those occasions on the trip when I found the red dirt roads. I hit a stretch of this red road after I left the park. There were few homes on the road so I was able to ride faster and standing up weaving to avoid any large rocks or holes. I left a plume of red dust behind and fortunately got a large amount on my bike.

I stayed on these backroads for a while until my computer convinced me I had run out of fun road and would have to return to the highway. It was time to return to the hotel and call it a day, but what a tremendous day it had been. High into the mountains to experience a measure of healing and back into the desert to appreciate a natural wonder and then visit the relics left behind by a man who thought he could permanently bend the earth to his will and almost did.

You should learn about yourself when you travel alone. For me, I was awakening on the road, coming back to the optimism and enthusiasm I had enjoyed before the dark days came. Maybe it was being higher in the mountains, I don't know, but I saw a lot of light up there at Cloudcroft and I saw it in a way that spoke to me.

For a man traveling alone, I was having a never-ending conversation, even if it was mostly with myself.

Chapter 12

Day Six

The Silver Lining

-----Original Message-----

From: Brian House
Sent: Tuesday, June 09, 2015 1:11 AM

As you can surmise by reading this, I did not go to Cloudcroft and camp. I have ended up in Silver City and I am glad I did for reasons that will become apparent as you read this installment.

This morning at the hotel in Alamogordo, I ran into one of the older fellows who had been admiring my GS the day before. He was a biker who had recently fractured his ankle and is currently off the bike. While his ankle ails him, his enthusiasm for riding remains. He again encouraged me to make the ride to "Silver" and said I would not regret the road (#152) through the Gila National Forest. I told him I would think about it and then I was off to do a few loads of laundry.

As I sat in the laundromat, I looked at my maps and decided I needed to do the Gila ride since it was early in the week. I decided to keep pushing west and then later in the week turn east and cover some of eastern New Mexico.

I left Alamogordo and went south on Highway 70 to Las Cruces. The best I can say about 70 is that it is efficient. Your life will not suffer if you never ride this road. Just straight four-lane at 75 mph. I reached Las Cruces quickly. It is an aerospace city with NASA's imprint everywhere. If you are inclined, there are museums and tours of the facilities. I had riding on my mind so I rode on.

I picked up Highway 185 on the outskirts of Las Cruces and rode the backroads for the rest of the day. If you wonder what really large scale agriculture is like, then you need to go out west and drive through some of this farm country. I crossed the Rio Grande numerous times today. That little river (it's a trickle compared to the Ohio or the Mississippi) supplies water for hundreds of thousands of acres of crops. Pecan orchards are everywhere as well as other crops which I did not know. Irrigation channels are everywhere. Water is the key to the economic survival of New Mexico as far as farmers are concerned.

At one point, I passed a farm that had dozens of the largest rooster boxes I had ever seen. These things were four-feet-tall and six-feet-long. "These guys are raising the biggest fighting chickens I have ever seen," I thought to myself as I rode. A little while later I saw many dozen more on the horizon, so I slowed to see just what these chickens looked like. I was about to stop when a Holstein dairy cow stuck her head out of one of the chicken boxes. The boxes were really heat shelters for dairy cattle. And I thought they were raising fighting chickens on steroids.

By early afternoon, I stopped for gas in Hatch, NM. I saw a little restaurant with some bikes parked in front. After gassing up I went back to the restaurant, which will remain nameless for reasons which will become clear, to have lunch. I met three bikers there who were from Great Britain. We talked for a few minutes and then they were on their bikes and gone. I liked the looks of this place so I decided to have one of their burritos. My waitress was the owner of the place. She was Anglo and straight out of a Woody Allen movie in a Diane Keaton, southwestern, LSD sort of way. She was very pleasant and conversant until her side of the conversation began to veer off beam. She ended up telling me and a few others she had recently bought a new house that was perfect for her and her two recently domesticated coyotes. They had taken to the place although her two monkeys were not sold on their new home as of yet.

Which put me to wondering...

How is it I have run into so many people who are just outright nuts on this trip? Is it them or have I inadvertently consumed something that has taken me on an altogether unplanned trip. My son says I am a dead ringer for the cartoon character Ned Flanders, so is it possible that when people see me they see this Ned guy and just proceed to yank my chain? I'm wondering...

I left monkey woman and headed for Route 152 and the Gila National Forest. The old gentleman was right. This is one heck of a road. I started out counting the curves, but quit at 100. It dawned on me that counting curves is a lot like asking someone how many acres they own or how much money they have saved for retirement. It's just rude. If you ride, just say it's a good road and that ought to be enough. Sorry if you have caught me counting curves before.

I hit 152 just as a storm was brewing. I found out later my British friends made it through before the storms. I got hit with its full force at 7,000 feet. It made those switchbacks and S-curves real work. I took my time and enjoyed the ride.

I made it into Silver City at supper time. When I pulled up to the newly restored Murray Hotel (also recommended to me by Old Gentleman), there were already 20-plus bikes parked out front. These were not your typical Harley's parked at the curb. Not one Harley. Not one. All were BMW GS's, Yamaha Super Tenere's, Honda Interceptors, Triumphs and other sport bikes. I even saw two scooters which were bad to the bone.

As I was dismounting, the three Brits came up to me and began quizzing me on my yellow Aerostitch gear. They really liked it, but confessed they still wore all black. Turns out they were part of a group of 23 Brits who had shipped their bikes to Key West and were riding from there to Prudhoe Bay, Alaska. These are some hardcore guys. All were in their late 50s to 70s. They were retired police officers, soldiers and lawyers. I liked these guys! They invited me to meet them at the pub down the street for dinner. I told them I would meet them there. This was one dinner date I was definitely going to keep.

After a quick shower off, I went to the pub where I had a jolly good time with Klempke (a diminutive Irishman who reminded me of the soldier types you see in old war movies), Sam and Dan. After a convivial beer or two, I asked Klempke what he thought of Charley Boorman. He shrugged and said, "I don't really give him much of a thought except that he's rich and he's Ewan McGregor's mensch." So much for diplomacy. Klempke then asked me if I knew who Nick Sanders was. I replied that I of course knew who he was and that he is the real deal when it comes to riding long and hard. Klempke said, "That's good because Nick is a close friend of mine and he's sitting right behind you." I turned around and sure enough, there sat Nick Sanders. Sanders, it seems, owns the tour company that puts on these tours and personally escorts them. Klempke would have none of it but to introduce me to Sanders. He was very gracious and willing to talk. I was wearing my "I'm Still Here Tour 2015" shirt and he wanted to know what it was. I explained to him that I was a cancer survivor and this ride was my celebration of life. He thought that was really cool. I got handshakes all around from the group and two of them accompanied me back to the bar to regale me about the four, count em', four speeding tickets one of them had received on the tour so far. Turns out he is an ex-detective from London, England and when he shows the "sheriffs" his badge, they throw the tickets away.

All in all, it was a lot of fun with my fellow riders from across the pond. I would have missed out on this experience entirely had I not listened to "Old Gentleman" and ridden to Silver City. I would also have missed out on monkey woman.

I'm not sure where I'm going tomorrow. Right now it is raining a flood that would float Noah's ark, so weather will have something to do with my plans.

Be safe and bless you all,
Brian

***   ***   ***   ***   ***

It was time for the Alamogordo portion of my ride to come to an end. I was ready to ride back up into the mountains at Cloudcroft, set up my tent, camp in peace and quiet and enjoy some bourbon and a good book for a few days, if not longer. I liked the high mountain air and the solitude the area offered. The fact that there were at least two restaurants in Cloudcroft that bragged about their biscuits and gravy along with sides of thick cut bacon would suit me just fine when I was inclined to leave camp.

I walked out of the Alamogordo Hampton Inn intending to load my gear and ride into the mountains. I had learned it took me a good 30 minutes to load up and gear up for a day's ride. The movies and TV shows that depict bikers just throwing a leg over their bike and taking off are nothing more than fantasy. There is no way to repack two side bags, a large duffle, load them onto the bike and properly cinch the duffle down in just a few minutes. It takes time to get them all to balance and the tension on the straps equally dispersed before turning your attention to gearing the body up with armor and water. I was efficient at it now for sure, but it still took time.

I noticed an older gentleman looking over my bike as I exited the lobby of the Hampton. I had talked to him the day before. He was retired Air Force and we got along great. He and his wife were standing by the bike, gazing at it as if it were a piece of art in a museum. That happened a lot on the trip. BMW motorcycles do not look anything remotely like a big Harley Davidson cruiser, so people stand around and try to figure out just what it is I am riding. Then there is the true breed, like this old gentleman, who actually own and ride BMW bikes. They get it. They embrace the far horizons of long distance riding and they select their bikes and gear for the intended purpose and not for the curb appeal needed at a local bar. He smiled at me as I approached and asked me where I was going today. I told him of my plans to ride up to Cloudcroft. He nodded his head and agreed that was a great idea, told me he was a BMW rider, but was currently recovering from a broken ankle courtesy of riding too fast off-road. He then politely suggested I ride over to Silver City and check it out at some point in my trip before I returned to Kentucky. He gave me the numbers of roads I should include in the ride to "Silver" so I could put the GS through its paces on some real curves should I chose to go. He told me to be sure and stay at the historic and recently renovated Murray Hotel should I go there. I liked this older fellow. He was a real gentleman, not presumptuous, just trying to help a fellow biker have a good ride. We shook hands and he and his wife got in their crossover vehicle and left the hotel parking lot. I went to my tank bag and pulled out one of my maps of New Mexico and started studying the routes that would take me to Silver.

There were two ex-Air Force guys sitting on the smoking bench by my bike. They had overheard my conversation with the older gentleman. I shook hands with the smokers and sat down to talk for a few minutes. They both agreed with the older fellow that Silver City should be on my agenda. They were Harley guys now, but the one with the goatee and the skull tattoo on his arm had owned a BMW in the past. I looked at my map for a few more minutes before putting them away and riding off to take care of my accumulated laundry.

The doing of very ordinary, pedestrian things can lead to real changes in plans. It did not matter where I wanted to go. The first thing I had to do was find a laundromat and do some laundry. Much to my disappointment, the quick dry fabrics of my underwear and socks were not all that quick dry, and since I had tried to wash them in sinks and dry them over air conditioner vents to no avail and things were really starting to smell bad, I decided it was time to actually break down and wash some clothes. The daily temperatures had run in the high 90s and at times well over 100, which meant all of my clothing was sweat-soaked and salt-laden. If I did not get busy and make my clothes clean, the nice folks at the Murray were not going to let me in their newly refurbished hotel should I decide to go there instead of Cloudcroft. I found a laundromat in a small strip mall just up Highway 70 on a side street from the hotel, so I rode up there to spend a few hours doing laundry and studying maps. Like so many times on this trip, it was the people who provided the greater focus for a dose of humility and opportunity for reflection.

I had not been in a laundromat since my college days some 37 years earlier. This one was as I had remembered those from the 1970s—tiled linoleum floor, four rows of coin-fed washers, some of which worked better than others. The washers were in the center of the establishment while banks of front-loading dryers lined the outer walls. There was a change machine and a detergent/fabric softener dispenser that sold those things to idiots like me who thought clothes just magically dried because it said so on the label.

Spend just 30 minutes in a laundromat, no, just spend 15 minutes in a laundromat, and if you are a privileged high income earner like me you will realize there are two Americas going on. There is my America, the one which has air conditioning and a security system for my home which sits in a subdivision with restrictions. There is my America which has excellent health insurance and top notch food. There is my America where my wife does not have to work. There is my America where I have time to have hobbies and write books and go to Africa and shoot the shit out of animals. There is my America where I have retirement accounts and fully-funded Social Security which, assuming cancer does not kill me, means I will have a nice retirement.

Then there is the other America. You can see it on the faces of the men and women who are in the laundromat. There was the black woman who was on the phone checking on her child who was earning money baby-sitting. She had walked to the laundromat carrying her clothes in plastic garbage bags. There was the old man washing his clothes in two machines and overloading both of them so he could save quarters for the dryers. An old white woman came in. She looked nervous and unsure. It was, I found out, her first time in the place. I wondered about her. Maybe she was newly widowed and, without her husband and his income, things had gotten harder for her than they had ever been. Maybe she was new to Alamogordo and this was just another in a lifelong succession of seedy laundromats that had been one of the weekly stations of her life. Whatever her story, she wore her uncertainty and anxiety on her face like a badge. The black woman caught it as quickly as I did. In a few moments, she made her way over to the old white woman and struck up a gentle conversation about the routine of doing laundry and the weather. She pointed out the washers that would steal your quarters and the dryers that worked really well. The old white woman relaxed a bit and then little by little she seemed at home in the place and soon settled down in one of the hard plastic chairs that are in these places and watched her clothes go round and round in the dryers.

The old man looked like cigarettes and drink had been at work on him for years. He was emaciated with leathered skin and bloodshot eyes. He sat alone and stared out the plate glass front windows. I doubt terrorists ever think to shoot up a place like a laundromat. I think they know the folks in here have already been forgotten by society.

There was a glue, a common, involuntary bond that seemed

to be the social fabric of the people in that place. It was tired and decades, perhaps centuries, old, but it was there and it was palpable. It was poverty and the despair that comes from the treadmill certainty that poverty would be there when each of them woke up tomorrow, if they woke up. These were people for whom society had no real use. There are no plans to help the adult chronically poor. They will live out the remainder of their grim lives on the margins. They are too old to get a job and they lack the education to fit into this digital age so they exist on the fringes of a society that has long since passed them by. They obey most of the laws most of the time. A black woman helps comfort and ease an old white woman. An old man stares out a window and wonders where his life has gone. These are the forgotten people that are part of our America.

I wondered whether these people had enough to eat for the rest of the week. Did they have safe shelter? Life is tough and for some it just stays tough until the day they die. It is not enough to preach a sermon to folks who are living in poverty. They need help, real substantive help to get out of the gutter that is poor food, minimal to no health care and substandard housing. Making those kinds of things happen is what church is for me. I do not ever want to be a part of a church that shuns the poor or supports a government that punishes the poor.

***   ***   ***   ***   ***

I finished washing my clothes and stepped outside to study my maps on my bike.

Well, what was I to do? Here I was on my ride with no set agenda. I was as free as a lark. I could go where I pleased, when I pleased. So what if I had declared yesterday that I was going to Cloudcroft to embrace my inner Thoreau on a mountain instead of a pond? I was free on the open road with no required agenda other than to ride back to Kentucky in a few weeks. The more I thought about it, the more Silver City seemed like my next destination. It would be another part of this trip I had not mapped out. Now if only the Murray Hotel had a vacant room. There are limits, after all, to reckless abandon. I looked up the Murray on my iPad and within a few minutes found myself talking to a pleasant lady who had just the room for me. She took my credit card info and with the miracle of that little piece of plastic, my shower and fresh sheets for the night were secure. I then turned my attention to my maps.

My Garmin said the trip would take three hours and cover 178 miles. The computer, however, did not know the national forest backroad, Highway 152, which the elderly gentleman had prescribed for me and which my new friends the retired Air Force guys had seconded as the only way to get there and have a good time. I looked at the route and it seemed to go through some pretty remote parts of the Gila National Forest and had some elevation to it. I didn't think it could be any worse than riding backroads in southeastern Kentucky so I guessed it would take an extra hour. I planned on getting into Silver by early to mid-afternoon and grabbing a fashionably late lunch there followed by a walk around town browsing the shops before finding a place to eat dinner that night.

All I can say is, the best laid plans, the best laid plans...

I pulled out of the laundromat parking lot and braked at the stop sign at Highway 70. It was my moment of truth. Turn right and I could still go to Cloudcroft. Turn left and I would be in seriously uncharted waters like so many other days on this trip. I waited for traffic to clear, eased off the clutch and throttled into a left turn heading south out of town. My decision had been made. It was time to ride into the unknown once again. Whatever Silver was I would find out after I covered roads that had never been in my plans during all the months of map study and community research. I was setting off on the words of an old guy with a broken ankle and two Harley dudes who might be laughing their heads off at me at that very moment.

***   ***   ***   ***   ***

The first two hours of riding to Las Cruces and a bit beyond were "big road," a state highway with speed limits at and in excess of 70 mph. While that sort of road and speed is great for trucks, commerce and just generally driving to a set destination, it is no fun for a biker like me. The wind gusts from passing and oncoming trucks require some getting used to and even then you end up getting blown about in your lane and sometimes out of your lane. I was glad when I had made it through Las Cruces, which is not to cast that city in a bad light at all.

Las Cruces, "The City of Crosses," is a city of about 100,000 people and the second largest in New Mexico. It is very much both Old Mexico and New Mexico in culture. The federal government is the largest employer. There is a noticeable aerospace presence in the city as you drive through. There are murals of astronauts and spacecraft and references to NASA. Spaceport America is nearby and Virgin Galactic, the world's first company to propose to sell sub-orbital spaceflights, has its headquarters there. There is a six-block downtown historic section of old Las Cruces that is full of shops, restaurants, old churches and numerous galleries. Normal people stop and take in all of that really nice stuff as part of their trip. Bikers like me, on the other hand, ride past it and hope for an open road.

It took me a few nervous minutes to locate Highway 185 that would lead me out of town. It seems my Garmin had not picked up on the heavy road construction in Las Cruces that re-routed the roads and made a spider's web of overlapping and narrowing lanes and unevenly distributed cones. I knew I needed to head northwest so I used the compass on the Garmin and needled my way in that general direction. I eventually saw the 185 sign and was much relieved. Soon I was free of the city and back among the rural landscape that I had found to be much more comforting than the congestion of the city.

Before I went to New Mexico, I had this notion that the state was just desert and red rock. Those things are there to be sure, but the reality is people can't make a living on just desert and red rock, the Ghost Ranch and Sedona, Arizona being well-known exceptions. The counties that generally make up the region around Las Cruces are agricultural in nature. The Rio Grande River meanders through this area, and while it is not at all a river like the Mississippi or even the Ohio, it is wet and it runs year-round which means it provides a reliable source of water for irrigation. This irrigation sustains large commercial farming enterprises. I am not a farmer so I am not qualified to comment on the benefits and evils of multinational corporate agribusiness. All I can say is I rode for mile after mile past farms that had large corporate signs erected prominently along the highway announcing to passersby the owner and operator of the farm. Most of what I saw were pecan orchards. I am sure there were many other crops there, but to an untrained eye moving along at 50 mph trying to guide a large motorcycle, the trees were the easiest to see and identify.

Heat is an ever present condition in the Southwest. Long sleeves and long pants and lots of body armor were my daily dress so I was always really hot out there, but I stayed hydrated and made it through with no trace of sunburn. When I saw the cows in their individual heat shelters, I knew that the livestock suffered just like the rest of us. Fail to protect your herd and you will find them all lying bloated and dead in your pasture. Seeing those cattle so individually well-provided for brought my mind back to the people in the laundromat and I wondered what kind of relief from the heat they had on those frequent and very typical hot desert days.

My ride to Silver was taking longer than I thought. I had slowed down frequently to gaze at the countryside and I meandered a time or two on sideroads to look at little communities that were no more than a post office and a two-pump gas station and garage. It was now early afternoon and I was running low on gas as I rode into Hatch, New Mexico. It took me a few minutes to find a gas station and then the search for food was on. I spotted a place downtown called "Sparky's" that looked like a good burger joint, but it was closed for the day. I had seen a little restaurant in a house near the gas station while I was getting gas. There were several motorcycles parked in front along the road. A sign denoting the place as a restaurant hung out front. It was a tidy looking place and had I not had my heart set on a hamburger it would have been my first choice. With my burger dreams dashed by Sparky's disappointing closure, I yielded to my now second choice and pulled in behind the other bikes. As I did so, three black clad bikers exited the establishment. They were, like me, older guys, the kind who should be able to behave themselves and if they do not they will not last long in a fight. It turns out these guys, blokes actually, were part of a larger group from Great Britain. We exchanged what I came to call weather pleasantries., i.e. "It's hot as hell out here!" and then they were off. I made my way up the short sidewalk and into the Mexican eatery which was very nice and very, very cool inside.

Owing to the off hour of my stop, there were only a few people inside dining. I picked a table and went about stripping off all my coats and hard armor. There was a thoroughly western man sitting nearby eating a massive burrito. He was wearing jeans, a checkered ranch shirt and a western hat made of straw. His western boots had toes so pointed he could have given vaccinations with them. He looked at me like I was from Mars, and I suppose I might as well have been given the layers of gear I had on in that heat. Still, he was friendly and greeted me with a smile and a sincere inquiry about my well-being. This proved to be a constant in New Mexico. People were universally friendly to me even if they did not understand my yellow banana coat and the armor underneath. I think it helped that I was always friendly and greeted everyone with a smile first. You learn to take people as you find them when you are on a bike. Solo motorcycle travel is a vulnerable way to see the world, and a biker just cannot afford to make enemies on the road.

Which brings me to what I will call the "Unusual People." Travel enough on the backroads of any country and you will get more than local flavor. You will run into people who just are not all there. These are the people town folks do not let get near the interstate because they know someone will pick them up as a joke and take them to a far off place and drop them off, perhaps so lost they will never be able to make it back home. I had already seen some of these vulnerable and out of touch souls in Eagle Nest and I was about to encounter another right here holding my giant burrito plate and can of Pepsi Cola.

The owner was also my waitress. I had high hopes for this place given its excellent air conditioning and cool tile floors. There was a professor from some regional university sitting at a back table. He was in his 40s and sporting the typical academic garb of well-groomed beard, round glasses, jeans and desert boots. He was regaling two young coeds with some professorial bullshit which they were more than willing to gobble up in the hopes of scoring an "A" in their summer course, while he no doubt was hoping to do a little scoring of his own. I turned my attention from him and ordered my giant burrito with hot green chili sauce on top from the owner.

As I noted in my diary, she was cute in a spacey, Diane Keaton/Woody Allen movie sort of way. She had the hair and a trim figure for a woman in her 40s. From where I was sitting, the professor should have been talking to her. His odds would have been much improved, but then, she wasn't taking his class. She efficiently took my order and brought me an ice cold Pepsi and a large glass of ice. I wanted a Diet Coke, but that is why they call this roughing it.

She moved on to talk to the professor and the cowboy hat man who had been nice to me. It was a one-sided conversation and it all came from her. She found it necessary, even vital that she go into considerable detail about her new domestic living arrangements. Turns out she was so very, very happy about buying her new house and finally getting to move in with her companions. It seems her two "recently domesticated" coyotes had just flat out fallen in love with the new digs. She was a bit down, though, because her two pet monkeys were not sold on their new home yet. I wondered how she knew what the coyotes were thinking. On the other hand, I had a pretty good idea how she knew her primate companions were not happy with their new digs.

Once when I was on safari in Africa, I convinced the young professional hunter who was trying to lead me around the Zimbabwean bush to stay out with me and let me hunt in the bush all day. This was a foreign concept for the fellow since he apparently thought you needed to take a nap in the middle of the day to kill stuff. I really did not care what he thought, and since I was paying an exorbitant rate to be there we were going to hunt during the heat of the day. We walked along a riverbed in the Sengwa River Valley looking for game. We saw a female bushbuck and some small rodents, but nothing worth our attention. We rounded a bend in the river, which at this time of the year was nothing more than a parched rock-strewn river bed, and there before us was a large nondescript tree just full of baboons. Hundreds of them. Baboons are amazing creatures. They are not particularly attractive when compared to the loveable chimpanzee I suppose, but they are family-oriented and they have a memory and are capable of passing down to the younger generation things they need to know. One of the things they apparently passed down was that humans who are approaching their tree are a very bad thing indeed.

When baboons want someone to go away, they have options. All smart creatures have options. Humans think they have perfected the options department, but after my encounter with these baboons I am not so sure. Baboons can attack a threat and are very well-equipped with their fangs and their brute strength, but to engage in combat means the males must leave the females and young babies of the troop in the tree alone. If they are attacked by a pride of lions, then the old divide and conquer stratagem comes into play. Baboons have learned not to give into the dividing your troops temptation. Custer could have learned from these red-rumped little fellows.

What baboons do when threatened in their roost is to defecate like mad. All of them. They just shit everywhere. Some take handfuls of the stuff and throw it out and away from the tree as far as they can. It seems lions, leopards and hyenas are particularly averse to baboon poo-poo. It smells exactly like human feces for all you non-Darwinists out there.

So, it was on my mind as I sat there probing the innards of my ground beef giant burrito whether this dear lady's monkeys had expressed similar displeasure toward her about their new home and whether she had obeyed health department regulations and washed her hands before preparing my meal. My guess is the professor knew all along this woman was eccentric and he was going to troll in cleaner, if not more productive waters.

I finished what was an excellent tasting burrito and got back on the bike to make my way to Highway 15. Whether I would contract E. coli from monkey poo-poo would be known a few hours later down the road. I was hoping for the best. As I rode, I could not help but consider monkey woman and the people I had met in Eagle Nest. Part of the gift of any ride is the people you meet along the way and so far I had met some real gems. It takes all kinds of people and their different perspectives to give the world the rich texture it deserves, and so far I was deep into the texture department.

***　　　***　　　***　　　***　　　***

I was soon on route 152. There was a sign of some kind posted just at the turn off warning motorists, something like, "Woe ye to all who enter here. There be dragons and you are on your own and just plain nuts for getting on this damned mess of a road." Or at least that's what I think it said. Or should have said. If they had ridden it like I rode it at 7,000 feet in blinding rain and hurricane winds.

The old broken ankle gentleman and my Air Force buddies had all assured me I would like this road. They were right. It was loaded with one curve after another. Real curves. The kind that belong on the hips of a really good-looking woman you can't take your eyes off of. I quit counting the curves at 100 and that was before I was finished with the initial ascent. This being a mountainous region, there is always an ascent followed by a descent. To hope for only one direction means you cheated on the trip. The curves were real leaners. I was beyond busy leaning hard and looking ahead for my next line, the place in the road I needed the bike to go to keep me from falling off the mountain. When you ride a motorcycle, you look ahead to your intended line of travel, not where you are but where you want to go. Let yourself be lured into looking down at where you presently are and you will crash and crash hard. So, here I was 100-plus curves into Highway 152 when Mother Nature decided to yank my chain. Down came the rain in buckets.

The rain changed things from exhilarating to butt-clenchingly scary. There are no guardrails to speak of on the road. I continued to climb and the rain persisted. There was no place to pull off so I was in the ride for better or for worse. I would get off this mountain or spend the night on it by the side of the road in my tent if I ever found a place to stop. At some point there had been a forest fire in the Gila. Forests recover from fires, and in many instances the fire serves as a rejuvenator for growth. The burned timbers leave lots of charred remnants and these flow onto the road in heavy rain. This makes the road slick and treacherous for bikers. More than once I had to navigate this black goo and do my best to stay upright as my tired body slipped and wiggled on the pavement. I was grateful for the absence of cars on the road. I was able to slow down to a snail's pace for several miles and make my way around some of the very worst of the roads. During the fire, some of the roads had contracted and melted with the extreme heat. The asphalt road surface in these areas was wavy and lumpy. Add to that the black charcoal sludge, the water and some nasty wind, and that was my road for many, many miles.

Hard as it may seem, I was having the time of my life out there. Every moment was cherished and just downright fun. To have come so close to letting this cancer get away from me to the point of no return, to now being out in a wonderful, wild place where nature set the rules was a gift beyond comprehension. I understand that dying in a Hospice unit may sometimes be necessary, but it is certainly not preferred. If I had been swept off that mountain that day in a torrent of black sludge and rain, it would have been heartbreaking for Susan and my children, but it would have been by far a better way to die than cancer. I celebrated every moment as I willed my way down that anonymous mountain.

The sky was red with the setting sun and I was hungry by the time I made the outskirts of Silver City. Silver is a town of about 10,000 people and is home to Western New Mexico University. I liked it from the moment I rode along the vintage 1930s-era downtown main street and parked across from the Murray.

$$*** \qquad *** \qquad *** \qquad *** \qquad ***$$

There are many ways to experience a cross-country trip. The fastest and most efficient is to travel by the interstate highway system. It is truly President Eisenhower's gift to the American people, and it makes America a much smaller place and provides for efficient movement of military personnel. It is also, in my opinion, absolutely the worst way possible to experience America. Real America. The soul of this place lies in the downtowns and backroads of our states. If you want to know who your neighbors really are, then get off the interstates—what we motorcyclists call "the slab"—and drive the old U.S. Highway system. These roads are well-maintained and will lead you through towns and cities and little villages. A cross country trip today of necessity means for most of us the interstate highway system, but once you are in your general vacation area it is by far better to leave the interstate behind and get off onto the backroads.

I pushed my kickstand down and killed the engine on my bike. I had been riding for hours and was glad to get off the saddle. I stood there admiring the elegant façade of the Murray. I looked to my right and realized there was another restored hotel on the same street just one block down. Parked in front of the other hotel were at least a dozen Harleys. Their riders were standing out front in their black leathers smoking cigarettes and admiring their bikes. One guy was smoking while using nasal cannula for his oxygen tank, which he carried slung over his shoulder at the same time. Nothing like maintaining a fire inches from the portal feeding you pure oxygen. He would have fit in with monkey woman and Mr. Witness Protection from Eagle Nest. Being detached from reality takes many forms and I was daily adding to my list ways I had observed people walking away from the reality I hope most of us are living in.

The vehicles parked in front of the Murray were a different

lot altogether. There, instead of the typical array of Harley-Davidsons, were about 20 adventure bikes like my own as well as sports tourers made by Honda and Yamaha. These are bikes that can go for thousands of miles and only need an oil change, while the Harleys are long since on the side of the road. People who ride the BMW R1200Gs, Honda VFR's, Yamaha Super Tenere's—these are riders who ride long distances and through all kinds of weather. We call ourselves Adventure Riders or long-distance riders, and while we do not dislike the Harley guys, we simply speak a different language and place a different emphasis on our hobby. We are very different people and both groups recognize the difference.

I angled my bike back into a parking space alongside the other adventure bikes and got off and walked toward the hotel entrance. As I neared the entrance I was greeted by three Brits who quizzed me about my riding apparel. Nice guys for sure and older riders like me. So what were the odds of running into two separate groups of British riders on the same day? As it turned out, they were from the same group as the men I had met at the Mexican restaurant earlier in the day. There were 23 of them all from the British Isles. They had shipped their bikes to Key West and were riding to Prudhoe Bay, Alaska as part of a guided tour. These guys were all in their late 50s to their late 70s. Most were retired police officers, judges, lawyers and soldiers. I liked these guys from the moment we started talking. They admired me for having the balls to wear a yellow banana bike coat across America. I was having fun just listening to them describe their bikes. I bent over to pick up my luggage and head into the hotel lobby when the Brits invited me to meet them down the street at the Toad Creek Brewery for a few beers and some dinner. I told them I would be there as soon as I got squared away.

Walking into the lobby of the Murray is like being on the set of *Casablanca* or some other Bogart movie set in an exotic locale. The lobby was painted a cool shade of yellow and was decorated with furniture appropriate to the 30s and 40s. It was all new or newly refurbished in excellent condition. Live ferns and other plants were situated around the lobby reinforcing the foreign country theme. The Murray saw to it that an ample number of chairs and couches were in the lobby. Art work and portraits of prior owners and community citizens of importance adorned the lobby walls. This was a lobby to sit down in and read the *Times* and discuss matters with a confidant. There was no need to hurry. Just sit down, relax and rest. The Murray will take of your every need.

The desk was staffed by the same young woman who took my reservation earlier in the day. She remembered me because of my "funny accent," which is to say I did not sound like her. Apparently I had a southern drawl, and although I contested that fact with her she laughed all the harder and kept saying, "Yes you do! Yes you do!" I good-naturedly gave up and took my key to go to my room which I found to be similarly restored and very clean. No bedbugs in the Murray!

I jumped in the shower and used my fair share and then some of the hot water the Murray was brewing up for its motorcycle guests. I felt my fatigue more when I was in the shower than any other time on the trip. I suppose it was the relaxing effect of the water, but whatever the reason I was pretty tired standing there in the Murray shower. Fighting my way over route 152 in that storm had been some work.

Dressed and refreshed, I made my way down the street to the Toad Creek Brewery. I walked past the Harley guys who were still outside smoking with the guy who was firing one up while hugging his oxygen canister bomb. They were not in the mood to talk to me, but they were Harley guys so I did not give it a second thought.

Every town needs a place like the Toad Creek Brewery. My hometown had a place like it called Weaver's until it burned down a few years back and the little town is just not the same. Towns need a good watering hole, a place where folks can go to laugh and cry, celebrate and commiserate with a beer or two or maybe three if the heartache is bad enough. Towns need a place like this where no one passes judgment and just lets life unfold at the bar and on the tables and couches that make up the landing zones for the patrons of the place. Beat up on their vacation, British and American bikers for sure need a place like the Toad Creek Brewery after days of hard riding, and tonight we were all happy patrons.

I walked up to the bar and found myself a seat. It was crowded and I ended up sitting between two groups of Brits. They were already in fine form and since I do not play catch up when I drink, they stayed well ahead of me all night long. The "Toad," as the Brits called it, is one of those modern beer joints that sells craft beers, some of which they brew on site. All I really wanted was a Coors Lite, but "when in Rome," so I ordered one of their craft beers which had a description that would do a $300 bottle of pinot noir worthy. I was so tired and so thirsty, dehydrated really from the ride, that any beer was going to suit me just fine. I ordered some fish and chips to go with the beer so I could start some salt back into my body and not fill up on beer which would leave me absolutely hammered in my dehydrated state. I played it safe and asked the bartender to bring me a glass of ice water as well.

I was working on my second beer and finishing my fish and chips when the Brit to my right introduced himself and asked me if I was a biker. I was wearing my "I'm Still Here Tour 2015" t-shirt so it was more or less a dead giveaway, but I replied that I was. We shook hands and there began my delightful conversation with my new friend "Klempke." He was actually an Irishman as he was quick to point out, and like most of the others he had been some sort of law enforcement officer back in Great Britain. We talked bikes and, like the other Brits I met that night, he was a hardcore rider with a serious penchant for fast sport bikes and a willingness to test the local American speed limits. Klempke introduced me to one of his mates who was a head taller than me, which made him two heads taller than the diminutive Klempke. They regaled me with their story of intentionally exceeding 100 mph repeatedly through some deserted area of west Texas earlier in the day only to be stopped by a Texas State Trooper who had actually drawn a gun on them. He ordered them to remove their helmets. When he saw they were in their 60s he exclaimed, "Hell! I can't arrest you guys. You're both old enough to be my grandfathers!" They got a good laugh out of that. The tall Brit told me he was collecting tickets on the trip and so far had more than anyone else in their group. He told me he had been a district criminal investigations officer back home. This was a grand adventure for them to be sure. They had started their ride in Key West, Florida and would, some six weeks later, finish it at Prudhoe Bay, Alaska at the end of the Dalton Highway. That is a dream ride for sure and a very, very long ride of over 6,000 miles. The fact that these older riders were attempting it and doing it on sport bikes for the most part just impressed the heck out of me. Most of us adventure bike riders are dismissive of sport bikes, but I became a convert that night and determined to add a sports tourer to my stable as soon as my dear wife would permit another bike in our garage.

My conversation with Klempke finally drifted around to great riders who have influenced our riding. I mentioned Ewan McGregor and Charley Boorman, the actors who made two real life motorcycle travel documentary films back around 2005. They both rode the BMW 1200 GS like I ride. It was their use of these bikes that fueled a lot of the adventure bike craze and inspired amateurs like me to buy these massive machines. I had watched both of their films repeatedly during the long winter months of riding my bicycle on its indoor trainer to build up leg strength for the ride. Klempke was polite about McGregor and Boorman, but diplomatically pointed out they were actors after all who had a support team. He then asked me if I knew who Nick Sanders was. I replied that I most certainly did. Klempke grinned and responded saying, "That's good mate, because he's sitting right behind you."

A word of explanation for you non-bikers out there is needed. Nick Sanders is what you would call "the real deal" when it comes to true round-the-world, long-distance adventure travel. The purists of the sport reserve that title for those brave souls who travel alone without any support team whatsoever and solve their problems as they go. This meant that Klempke and his mates knew they were just tourists having a good time. In a small way, I met their definition of adventure rider because I was out on the road far away from home and doing it on my own, although never so far that a credit card could not get me out of a jam. Nick Sanders, by comparison, goes places where the people who live there have no idea what a credit card's real use is. He has ridden around the world seven times and up and down the Americas seven times, all as a solo rider. He holds the world record for riding around the world faster than anyone else. His list of accomplishments goes on and on. So when my drinking buddy Klempke told me Nick Sanders was sitting behind me, I was sure he was joking.

Only he was not. I turned around and there sat Sanders having pleasant conversation with some of the other Brits. I was shocked. It would be like mountain climbers meeting Sir Edmund Hillary. Klempke could see the surprise on my face and he grinned from ear to ear before informing me that Sanders was leading their expedition. He was their tour operator and was taking care of all logistics, luggage transport, medical care and shipping of the bikes.

"Would you like to meet him?"

"You bet I would."

"Let's have a go then. He's a great chap."

Klempke took me over and made the introductions. There were five or more other Brits sitting there with Sanders. After a few pleasantries, Sanders looked at my t-shirt and asked me what kind of tour I was on. I explained to him it was a one-man tour and I was the one man, and that I was riding across America to celebrate still being alive after having had prostate cancer.

Maybe it was just the cancer thing. Maybe it was the fact that it was prostate cancer and I was with a bunch of older guys like me for whom the fear of prostate cancer is always there. Whatever it was, my little one man "I'm Still Here Tour 2015" really resonated with all of them. Suddenly, it was three cheers for me and handshakes all around. Sanders and I continued talking for a few minutes before two of the Brits insisted on taking me back to the bar for a round of drinks to celebrate kicking cancer's ass. I was more than happy to oblige.

Klempke told me the group would ride north toward Monument Valley the next day and I had been invited to tag along for as many days as I wanted. It sounded like a great idea to me. I told him I would give it some thought and study my maps to see if I could make it work. He and the other Brits left shortly after that because they said they had an early morning. I bid them good night and sat at the bar for a while longer nursing that final beer and savoring the handshakes and congratulations I had received from my new friends.

It helps to have support when dealing with any form of adversity. It helps no matter the source. Here I was in the "Toad" and I had been encouraged and affirmed in my fight and quest to live by a bunch of retired policemen. I felt alive and I had hope. How could I not have hope sitting here in this little brewery strong and healthy and full of purpose. I was everything cancer had tried to take away and I had denied it entry. It was my plan to keep the door closed to cancer for the rest of my life.

I walked out of the Toad into the cool desert night air. It was dark and the air smelled of rain. I walked along the main street doing the window shopping I had meant to do that afternoon. The stores were filled with interesting artwork and jewelry. I made a note to bring Susan back here on one of our visits to see our son. I walked back to the Murray. A breeze was starting to blow, but I did not see any clouds in the sky so for the first time on my trip I did not cover my bike with its rain cover.

I spent a few minutes at the front desk talking to a traveling salesmen who wore hearing aids. His batteries must have been losing their charge because he kept repeating his questions. He was intrigued about our bikes and I patiently answered his questions. He told me about my breakfast options around town for the next day. I thanked him and then begged off further conversation and headed to my room to get some sleep. I knew I had at least an hour of writing ahead of me as I kept my journal of the trip and that would make for a late night anyway.

The Murray, being a vintage hotel, had windows you could actually raise, and since the windows had screens in them you knew you were allowed to let in all of the night air you wanted. Silver City sits at almost 6,000 feet so nights are cool anyway. I raised the window and went to work writing. I was exhausted by the time the last words were written. I turned off the light and laid down on the bed above the covers, letting the breeze blow over me. It had been a great day, one of the best of my life. I closed my eyes. My slumber was interrupted by jarring thunder and the crack of lightning right on top of me.

It came a flood.

I left my bike uncovered for the first time and it came a flood.

I rolled over in bed and let the rain come down.

I would worry about it tomorrow.

Chapter 13

Day Seven

A Day of People, Signs and Bugs

-----Original Message-----
From: Brian House
Sent: Wednesday, June 10, 2015 1:55 AM

I did a lot of New Mexico riding today. 355 miles and I never left the Land of Enchantment. I really enjoyed my stay at the Murray Hotel in Silver City. It has a retro 1940s look, but with thoroughly modern conveniences.

My day started at 6:45 this morning. I was still in bed when I was awakened by the roar of 20-plus bikes tearing out of town. I started laughing, thinking of those Brits, all my age and older, flying out of town determined to wake me up and break every speed limit in the state.

I tried to get out of town early, I really did, but it seems when people see a lone biker people want to talk. The first was a 60-something guy on a Surly mountain bicycle with extra-large tires. He asked me about my bike and I in turn asked him about his since I have a Surly Long Haul Trucker steel frame touring bike. He was pleased to know I will pedal and he in turn told me he owned a GS, an older model. He was wearing a baseball hat under his biking helmet and had a classic vintage 60s scraggly beard. I took him for a draft evader, but in the course of our conversation I learned he was retired U.S. Navy having worked in sonar tracking of Soviet subs. He finally said to hell with the Navy and has been in New Mexico ever since. Those were his words. He asked me where I was going and I explained my general clockwise loop toward Lincoln. He offered to retrieve his old *maps and show me some route options. He left on his bike and I resumed trying to load my bike.*

At that point a van pulled up alongside me. The middle-aged white male driver was another BMW enthusiast who wanted to show me pictures of his BMW. It was the model used in an old James Bond film. I'm sorry, I can't remember the model. We stood there talking bikes when Sam, the Navy man came pedaling up. I bid the van fan good day and sat down on the sidewalk with Sam and studied maps. It was one of those great, spontaneous moments that make solo travel so fulfilling. I had totally misread this man. Here he was, a veteran going out of his way to help me. He ended up giving me his map. We shook hands and off he went.

I finally got away shortly before 10:00 a.m. My route took me up scenic Highway 180 into the Gila again. I made a right at Reserve, NM and rode the high country for the rest of the day. I crossed the Continental Divide at an elevation of about 7,250 feet. Along the way I stopped to admire some of the scenery of the Gila Wilderness. When it was set aside as a wilderness, it was large enough that a man could ride in one direction on a horse or a mule for two weeks and never see another person. That's a big piece of real estate.

Backroads travel takes you to some really out of the way places. I stopped for gas at the Glenwood Trading Post. It was the only real viable business in this tiny wide spot in the road. The inside of the store was right out of the Great Depression, and I'm not talking about the Cracker Barrel Country Store nostalgia version. The place was dimly lit and much of the interior was cluttered with what I think had been someone's long ago effort at stocking a variety store only to see that venture fail and leave the merchandise to wither and decay. The good news for me was a shelf stocked with Payday candy bars that were not out of date. I grabbed a couple of Paydays, paid for my gas and was on my way.

Once again I found the only thunderstorm in New Mexico and managed to ride in it for an hour. The temperature dropped from 88 to 51 and stayed there for quite a while. It may be a desert, but it still rains out here.

I passed some signs today that put me to thinking about the mental state of the people who come up with these things. The first was a state highway sign that said "Do not drive on wet oil." Hmmm...I wondered as I was whizzing along around a curve going 65, "Am I about to die? Is the road up ahead covered in black goo that will spell my doom? Could it be the prison inmates just had too much time on their hands and made a bunch of these and the state had to put them somewhere?" I rounded the curve and found dry blacktop. Score one for the inmates.

Next up was a sign that really made me feel bad for the youth of tiny Magdalena, NM. I was cruising carefully down their main street at 25 mph so the speed trap police officer parked under the tree would not have an excuse to write me a ticket when what did I see but the local high school and a sign in its yard that said, "Home of the Magdalena Steers." Think about it for a minute. I get using bulls or stallions for a mascot, but a steer? Just imagine the trash talk, the smack going down across the line of scrimmage. The poor, castrated Steers of Magdalena are never going to live it down. They should find the principal who presided over such stupidity, and if they have already fired him they should rehire him just so they can fire him again for coming up with the Steers thing.

Late afternoon found me in Carrizozo, a town you may not have heard of before. It is important because it was the location of the rail depot that put Lincoln out of business after all of the Billy the Kid troubles in the Lincoln County War. I can't tell that Carrizozo prospered much from putting the hurt on Lincoln. Still, I was tired and there was a motel there and I thought I would get a room.

I should have been warned off by the owner having her charcoal grill going right by the front door. I should have heeded the smeared and dirty fly swatter on the counter, but I didn't. I asked if there was a room available. (There was a good chance there was since mine was the only vehicle in the parking lot.) "Why yes, yes there is," said the diminutive Indian lady, and it could be mine for $37.50 cash and no receipt coming back my way. The place was entirely off the books. Still, I gave the little lady my cold hard cash and got a key, a real key, to Room #3. As I walked the 10 steps from the lobby, being *careful not to get burned on her grill, I noticed two Indians in a worn out pickup driving slowly by my bike and looking it over good. These were not men who would have what it takes to buy one, but they would definitely have what it takes to steal mine. I decided to use at least some of my little grey cells and check the room out before unloading the bike. I did think of that. Did you know dirty motel rooms can have bedbugs? They can have them in the bed, on the walls and on the furniture. They can also have ants crawling all over the walls. Yes, I hit the jackpot here. My Room #3 had them both in abundance. I threw the key on the bed and walked out and got on my bike. By then another guy was walking around my bike. I decided to donate the $37.50 to little Indian woman and her grill and get out of there.*

Forty-five minutes later I pulled up to a certain chain hotel in Ruidoso. I had looked at its advertisement on my mini-iPad and found that their rooms had been remodeled in 2012. Things were looking up. I walked in and waited for the desk clerk to help the woman who walked in just as I did. Their conversation went like this:

Woman: "Do you have any rooms?"
Clerk: "Yes, we have plenty. What kind do you want?"
She got her room.

Then it was my turn:
Me: "I would like a room."
Clerk: "We don't have any."

As you might imagine, I did not take this lying down. We exchanged a few more pleasantries and the best the desk clerk could come up with was they did not have a room in my price range. I know what you're thinking: she knows I'm poor because my bike and its doo-dads only cost $30,000. No one drives cars that cheap anymore. I persisted and told her to give me what they had. She said it was too expensive. I finally laid my cards on the table: "Miss, you don't have anything in this place that I can't afford so give me a room now." I am proud to report I am writing this blog tonight in a deluxe double queen suite with a pullout bed and desk area, all for $109.00. After *she quoted me the rate, I asked her if they took AAA.*

*"Why yes sir we do," she said sweetly, "but I took one look at you
and gave you the Senior Citizen Discount."*

Score one for her. You can't win them all.

*I like the rough and tumble and the unexpected, and I seem to get it
all out here. Sam the Navy man was so helpful and even little Indian
woman helped me by giving me the opportunity to hone my bedbug
skills. Finally, anti-biker clerk was the most instructive of all
because she made me feel, in some much less significant way, what a
black person or a gay person feels like when the door is slammed in
their face. Stuff like that is wrong on any level.*

*I don't know where I'm going tomorrow. I'm thinking of taking out
an ad on T.V. here to offer my services to end droughts. Just call me
and the rain will follow.*

Be safe and bless you all,
Brian

***   ***   ***   ***   ***

I never saw the Brits again. I went to sleep to the sound of heavy
rain, content with having completed a day of challenging riding and
a fun night at the Toad. I gave some thought to joining up with the
Nick Sanders troupe, but in the end I decided I had started out on a
solo journey and I wanted to see it through to the end as a lone rider.
I had studied the map some after I made it back to the room and I
looked at it again in the morning in the hotel restaurant as I enjoyed
a very fine cup of coffee and a bagel. Nick Sanders was in the room
with one of his employees discussing the route their support vehicle
would follow for the day. While he is an adventurer of the first
order, his beginning the day conversation with his staff revealed him
to have the same ordinary concerns and logistical issues as any other
traveler, i.e. how do we get from here to there as safely and cost-
effectively as possible?

    I looked at my New Mexico map and mentally traced the

route I would have to follow north if I wanted to reach Utah in a few days. I had more than enough time to do it and I was assured of being in the company of some really fine people. But…I wanted to be alone and do this by myself.

This was part of my survivor's journey, the need to tell myself over and over again that it is possible to endure the hardest of things alone just because it has to be done and then to survive it and do other things alone as part of the process of making peace with the hell that had been my life. That hell may come again, but now I know I can endure it through to the end. I would finish this ride alone and enjoy the freedom it afforded me with every rising and setting of the desert sun.

I checked out of the Murray with a twinge of regret. I really could have done with a full day in this wonderful town and another night at the Toad, but I vowed to return soon. I gave my key to the morning desk clerk and walked my gear out onto the sidewalk to load the bike. The rain had soaked my sheepskin saddle cover, but wonder of wonders, just a hard shake of the sheepskin and it was free of the moisture and I had at most a slightly damp saddle. I unlocked my hard case side luggage and started the process of once again carefully packing for the day's ride. I wanted to be out on the road for my ride around northwestern New Mexico as soon as possible. It was not going to happen. People were going to happen and they were going to keep me in Silver for a bit longer than I had planned. There was a time when these pleasant interruptions would have bothered me. Now I regard them as part of my pastoral evolution, the journey I am making as a minister and a survivor.

Sometimes I am asked when I "became a minister." It is not an easy answer. I would like to be one of those people who could claim a lightning bolt from God hit me and an angel told me to become a minister. I would take a Damascus road experience where, like the Apostle Paul, I was blinded as I made my way along some road and was told by Jesus to get ready to go to work for him. It did not happen that way for me. I came to the ministry gradually, seeking and searching and yearning to be close to God and then realizing there was this emptiness in me that was only filled when I was caring for people in my role as a minister. If there is a feeling of vocational wholeness in one's job, then I can say I only truly feel that wholeness when I am serving in a pastoral capacity. What has been the most amazing and humbling thing to me are those moments in my life when I become aware I am interacting with someone in a pastoral capacity. It does not always happen when I am wearing my robes and stole. More frequently, indeed the majority of the time, I am dressed in ordinary clothes just doing my ordinary thing and then suddenly, as I am talking with someone it will hit me—I am God's minister, his hands and feet on earth. I am capable of extending his love and grace to this person with whom I am talking, but it is entirely up to me whether I choose to put forth God's love for that person to see and hear and touch. In saying that, I do not mean to suggest I am proselytizing and thumping a Bible while talking to someone. It is actually quite the opposite. I find myself just talking to folks, listening to them, slowing my day down and setting aside my personal agenda in order to make time for them, to listen to their story and accept them for the person of worth that God regards them to be. In those moments, I am a minister again in the journey that is my life. What a church hierarchy might call me, I do not know and I certainly do not care. I know I am a minister and I have learned ministry takes many forms and not all of them are inside the four walls of the church.

I had parked my bike across the street from the Murray under a street light for security reasons. By happenstance, the sidewalk was elevated some two or three feet in that area which made for a nice loading platform and a convenient place to sit, which is what I was doing as I sorted through the soft bags that I would load into the hard-sided aluminum cases that carried my gear. I was moving around the bike and the cases when I noticed a man riding up to me on a hybrid bicycle. It was an older steel frame design bike with fat off-road tires. I have a bicycle very similar to it and enjoy riding it weekly. The fellow was wearing a baseball hat under his bike helmet and he had salt and pepper hair which hung down over his ears. He sported a scraggly beard right out of the campus unrest of the 60s. The man waved at me, said "Good morning," pulled over and came to a stop beside me. I returned the good morning and there began a conversation that was generated by a love of all things two-wheeled.

I assumed incorrectly this "Baseball Hat" man was some radical from the Vietnam War era who had walked away from society. I was only partially right. He was old enough that Vietnam applied, but he was retired Navy and anything but a war protestor.

He was enjoying his retirement as far away from the United States Navy as he could possibly get, hence his logic in deciding to make his retirement home in the high desert of southwestern New Mexico. Baseball Hat Man was also a GS rider and he wanted to give my bike a good looking over. He was fascinated by the upgraded electronics and technology since his bike was a much older model. I explained to him the electronics could be problematic, but you could see the gleam in his eye. He was in love with the new machine.

We both sat down on the sidewalk to talk. He wanted to know where I had been and where I was going. He had seen the Brits storm into town the night before and had read the newspaper article in the morning paper that they were on their way north. I told him I had been invited to tag along for a few days and had considered it, but had resolved to go it alone and keep riding in New Mexico. He asked me if I had a route planned. When I told him no, just a general direction toward Lincoln, New Mexico, he said, "Sit right here and I'll be back. I'll go get my maps for you." Off he went on his bicycle pedaling back the way he came. I did not know if I would ever see him again so I returned to my work.

I should say, I tried to return to my work. While I had been talking to Baseball Hat Man, I noticed a maroon van pull up alongside my bike. A middle-aged man was sitting in it behind the steering wheel just staring at my bike. I gave him a smile and a wave and he pulled his van even closer before speaking to me:

"Is that a GS?"

He was just about to salivate out the window and drool on his driver's door.

"Yes. A 2015."

"I've got one too. It's an older model. They used one like it in a James Bond film. I don't ride it much. Here, come look. I keep pictures of it on my phone."

In no time at all, the two of us were hunched over his phone screen oohing and ahhing over each of his dozen or so pictures of his bike as if it were his firstborn son. Our conversation and photo session were just concluding when Baseball Hat man came pedaling back up the street. True to his word, he had ridden back home and retrieved his maps. We then resumed our improvised seats on the sidewalk and began looking at the maps. Van Man said goodbye and was off and away to begin whatever his day in Silver held for him.

Baseball Hat Man had marked routes on his maps with a highlighter and a pencil and made suggestions relative to scenery and difficulty of the roads. I did my best to make mental notes of the detailed conversation, hoping I could mark some of these on my maps when he left. He concluded his instructions by folding up the maps and handing them to me,

"Here. Take these. You'll need them to find your way."

"But those are your maps," I protested.

"It doesn't matter. You're the one making the ride today. I'll get another map when I need one. You need a map today."

I was close to speechless. We shook hands and he was off, pedaling down the main street of Silver going to his job, and here I stood with his well-worn and well-marked-up maps. I am as possessive of my maps as I am of my books. For a seasoned traveler to part with one of his veteran maps was a true act of grace and kindness. I think both of us were ministers in that moment. I, the lawyer turned minister, and he, the sailor turned desert retiree. It was a good moment.

***   ***   ***   ***   ***

My discussions with my retired Navy buddy provided me with two options. The first was what riders call a "there and back" route which involved me riding to the Gila Cliff Dwellings National Monument north of Silver City. This ride would require me to retrace my route back to Silver at the end of the day. I knew these ancient cliff pueblos would be spectacular, but since I had seen similar structures in my earlier travels to Mesa Verde and Chaco Canyon years ago, I opted for the second route which was to proceed west and northwest from Silver City on U.S. Highway 180. This route would take me through the Gila National Forest as well, but provide me the option of riding into Arizona or swinging eastward along several points, should I choose, and then ride back across New Mexico.

I rode out of town around 10:00 a.m., vowing to return someday. Silver City had been a great experience, but there was more to discover on the road ahead. Like most U.S. highways, 180 was in excellent condition. I was free from town within just a few minutes and back riding into rural New Mexico. I came to look forward to the rhythm of my morning rides. The coolness of the air at the beginning of the day and the soft light of the rising sun were an invitation to leave a place I really liked and move on to find something new. This morning's ride was particularly beautiful given the effect of the heavy rains of the evening before. The ground was moist and everything had a touch of lingering rain resting on the surface for a few more minutes before being burned off by the inevitable midday sun. The road offered up gentle curves and changes in elevation that kept my attention. Gone were the miles upon miles of straight asphalt I had ridden in eastern New Mexico. Here in the southwestern part of the state I had to pay attention as I rode into the wilderness and began climbing in elevation and encountering more mountainous terrain. There was very little traffic on the road that morning, and I doubt there is ever a lot of traffic on the road the farther it takes you into the wilderness. There is a reason they call it wilderness. No one is home for hundreds of square miles.

I had been riding for about two hours when I came to the tiny community of Reserve. It is a small community of about 300 folks who run a few groceries, hardware store and most importantly, a bar that serves food. It is the county seat of Catron County, which is New Mexico's largest and least populated county.

Reserve is historically significant because it is the place where lawman Elfego Baca held off a gang of cowboys who tried to kill him for arresting cowboy Charles McCarty. Baca was one tough lawman. According to legend, some 80 cowboys attacked him as he holed up in an adobe structure. Over 4,000 rounds were fired at Baca, yet none struck him. Baca killed four of his attackers and wounded eight others before agreeing to surrender into the custody of a fellow lawman. He was subsequently tried and acquitted for killing some of his attackers. During the trial, the door to the adobe that was Baca's fort was introduced into evidence. It had over 400 bullet holes in it. Apparently the jury felt that any man who could endure such an onslaught deserved to go free. This little fight is remembered as the "Frisco Shootout" since Reserve in those days was known as "Middle San Francisco Plaza." Later in life, Baca became a successful trial lawyer. He still carried a gun and fought more gun battles. He would have fit right in with the lawyers of southeastern Kentucky.

It was noon when I came upon Reserve so, spying the little

restaurant, I pulled in and got off my bike. The gravel parking lot was full of pickup trucks and a few white Suburban's bearing U.S. Government license plates. If working men were eating here, it was going to be good food.

The first thing I saw after walking into the little, one-story, wooden-framed establishment was a sign handwritten by the owner offering to sell the place. Seems they needed to go to a bigger town and were tired of cooking all the time. I'm usually pretty wary of eating in places where the cook is unhappy, but I looked around and saw that the place was full and people were happy and having a good time. There was a table of six Hotshots, the parachuting firefighters who defend our forests when fire breaks out, eating their lunch and they looked satisfied. Since those young people do real work for a living, I figured they weren't going to eat anywhere that would make them sick so I decided to give the menus a go. I decided to play it safe and ordered a hamburger and fries, my reasoning being that even an unhappy cook cannot screw up a beef patty and some potatoes dumped in a vat of boiling fat.

I took off my yellow gear, but for once I was in similar company since the Hotshots had garments dyed the same Hi-Viz yellow lying around the floor by their chairs. No one even gave me a second look when I sat down at my table. I had picked out a table in the back by a window so I could watch what was going on outside, and in truth it was a pretty quiet place. Just a few vehicles rolling by. A black and white cur dog sat on the ground looking around at his surroundings. Apparently he mattered to someone because he sported a red nylon collar and had been tied to a nearby tree with a piece of cotton rope. I guessed his owner was sitting in here somewhere near me having lunch. The dog did not seem to mind in the least which suggested to me he had been through this routine before.

The waitress brought me my food and drink. It seems the red plastic Coca-Cola cups are ubiquitous in the west. Everywhere I went, I drank out of a red Coca-Cola cup even if the restaurant no longer served Coke products. I took my time eating and enjoyed listening to the friendly banter of the Hotshots. These were young people on the cusp of their lives doing something very dangerous, but very exciting. At their age, it is the excitement they latch onto. Their physical vigor and their relative lack of experience with death afford them the comfort of the illusion that nothing bad will happen to any of them. I think I was like that once. Now I live with the knowledge that the bad, the pain and injury, the dying and death are all out there waiting for each of us in appropriate measure. The key to living a full life is to not dwell on these things since they are ultimately unavoidable in one form or another and instead just go on living. Time and age bring us all to a place where being a Hotshot is no longer possible, but we can live within our world and have a Hotshot's attitude and take the chances, embrace our lives and move forward with desire not fear as our guide.

I paid my bill and decided to head east deeper into the Gila Wilderness. I would be riding in the high country for the rest of the day. I started climbing again and at some point I crossed the Continental Divide at an elevation of 7,250 feet. I would cross it several times that day as my route meandered through this quiet and lonely place.

To understand just how alone a person can be in the Gila, it helps to know how its boundaries were originally established. The great ecologist Aldo Leopold persuaded the Forest Service to set aside the Gila as a wilderness area in 1924. It was our country's first designated wilderness. In its original designation, it consisted of 755,000 acres and was wild enough that a person could travel on horseback for two weeks without seeing another person. I stopped several times to gaze upon the vast expanse of forest and mountains that is the Gila and I have no doubt the old maxim of two weeks without seeing another person still applies. Periodically, I would see rain in the distance rolling down from the mountains and with the dark storm clouds at times bumping into the face of the ranges. Nature is random and unpredictable anywhere, but in remote country it bears close watching when traveling alone since a heavy flash flood or a lightning storm can be disastrous for the solo traveler. I rode through a few mild showers over the next few hours, but for the most part I rode slowly with my visor up, just inhaling the sweet aroma of the high alpine air as I rode along.

By mid-afternoon I needed gas and something to eat. Riding a heavy bike around makes for a persistent hunger. I found gas and food at the Glenwood Trading Post. While it has seen better days, it is still a functioning part of the community, providing fuel and some basic food staples to people who stop by. Much of the inventory was old and constituted more of the antique and curio variety than current, useable food and dry goods. What was current and very much useable were the Payday candy bars sitting on a shelf. I availed myself of two of these as well as a soft drink, paid for them and my gas and hit the road.

I am always more comfortable on the road with a full tank of gas. Traveling fully fueled and with my two spare gas canisters gave me a range of 300 miles. That is a long way even out west. I pointed the GS east on Highway 12 and turned the throttle. It was not long before I rode into a heavy thunderstorm. The temperature dropped from 88 to 51 in a matter of minutes. Wind and rain came by the bushels and I was fine with both of them. The more you ride, the easier it is to ride in the wind. The same for rain. I had great waterproof gear so I stayed dry. What always concerned me was the lightning. Motorcyclists are very vulnerable to being struck and killed by lightning. I was vigilant watching for approaching lightning. Here, unlike other places earlier in my journey, I could dismount and get away from the bike if lightning approached. Fortunately, none did, and I was able to ride out of the bone-chilling storm and back into the heat of a New Mexico summer.

***　　　***　　　***　　　***　　　***

Signs are a big part of travel. It does not matter whether the traveler is on an interstate, a backroad or a hiking trail, all signs exist for a reason and travelers see them and if they do not rely on them, they at least absorb the information and try to interpret their intended meaning. I learned that signs are not always accurate or relevant so it paid to read each one with the eye of a skeptic.

At one point riding through the Gila I come upon a sign that read, "Do not drive on wet oil." This tells me there is wet oil ahead and that it is a very bad idea for me to take my rubber-tired vehicle across a road with oil on it. Since I think most, if not all, drivers already know this, I conclude this must be an imminent warning of a deadly, oil-slickened road ahead. Since the sign is placed on my side of a blind curve and I'm breaking the law doing 65 mph, I conclude there is oil and death waiting for me on the far side of the curve. Bracing myself for an unmanageable road, I ride on only to find a road as dry as the rest. No oil. No nothing. Maybe there had been oil in the past and maybe there will be oil again, but as it was the sign was just a public service announcement that did nothing but raise my blood pressure.

I came to the end of Highway 12 and turned due east onto U.S. Highway 60. I had decided to ride back to the Alamogordo/Ruidoso area and camp for a few days in the high alpine forests like I had intended to before my very pleasant Silver City detour. Little towns have a way of just popping up when riding the backroads. There are no green and white interstate signs that point the way, but there are still those pesky mind-numbing signs that make you wonder what people were thinking.

Take the sign denoting the school mascot of Magdalena, New Mexico high school. It is another of the many small towns that form the backbone of America and that we cannot do without. Having said that, the school officials in charge of the nickname, well, if I could have scratched my head through my helmet I would have done so.

I could tell Magdalena wanted to increase its municipal coffers with some speeding ticket revenue by the 25 mph sign at the city limits followed by the police cruiser sitting under a tree not too far in the limits. I got the GS down to a very legal 25 mph and took my time riding through town which is not very big, but it does have the aforementioned high school. There on the grounds of the school rising above the building on a pole of some kind is their sign which denotes the campus as "The Home of the Magdelana Steers." Steers. Nothing like playing your heart out for a mascot who has had his nuts cut off. Just imagine going to play an away game against another team and the grief the players no doubt receive because they are the nutless wonders. Whoever the crew was that decided to make castration the focal point of their mascot needs to step back and revisit the whole point of the mascot thing. Lamb fries and sterility are not part of a collective successful group identity. The name is certain to drive away residential development. Who wants to go to a place where they cut your nuts off and celebrate the mutilation by making a meal of the discarded parts?

***　　　***　　　***　　　***　　　***

It was getting late in the afternoon when I pulled into Carrizozo. I had ridden further east to the end of Highway 60 and picked up U.S.

Highway 380 to continue my eastern ride. Carrizozo is now little more than a four-way intersection of roads. Back in the time of Billy the Kid, Carrizozo was famous as the rail depot that put Lincoln, New Mexico out of business after the Lincoln County War that made him famous. Today, there are a few restaurants, some gas stations and some small motels. I was tired and ready to stop. The Kid probably stopped there from time to time, so I figured I could as well.

Traveling successfully means traveling with your eyes wide open and using all your senses. Just because you want something does not mean you get to have it when you want it. Just because you need something does not mean you are going to find it. What I wanted was a nice clean room, a hot shower and some food that would be better than the simple burger I had for lunch. Standing at the gas pumps with the wind howling all around me, I saw two motels. Both had 15 or so rooms and appeared to have been built in the 1950s. Both had recently seen some fresh paint and my hopes were high that things were going to work out. I picked the one on the side of the road with the gas station and rode to the door that had a sign above it that said "Office." Underneath that sign was another sign that read "Vacancy." I got off the GS and walked to the door, taking care not to bump into the charcoal grill with fired up briquettes in it sitting next to the office door.

I should have stopped right there. Should have turned around, walked back to my bike and ridden on, but I was in the trance of fatigue and getting beaten up on the road that comes with riding through wind and rain and altitude for hours. The lobby was little more than a gathering place for the owners to use before walking into their living quarters located in some unseen rooms behind the wall. Old calendars and faded prints hung on the walls. There was an old fly swatter on the counter still harboring the remains of some very smashed and disemboweled flies on its webbing. I still proceeded to ask if a room was available.

The little lady on the other side of the counter assured me there was in fact a room for me and it could be mine for the night for just $37.50 cold hard cash. I gave her the money and she gave me a key and no receipt. This place was off the books in so many ways.

I stepped aside into the afternoon heat, taking care not to run into the grill. Mine was the only vehicle in the parking lot, but at least I had a key to a room. At that moment, two Indians pulled up in a worn out pick-up and stopped behind my bike. They began pointing at it and gesturing to one another. Their truck cost maybe what my bike's tires cost, but it could sure haul my bike off when they returned to steal it in the night. Still, I thought, "I might be just too suspicious of these gentlemen. Perhaps they are just BMW owners who put all their money into their bikes and not into their truck or their dental care."

Something in me woke up when I saw the Indians driving away and the one riding shotgun was looking out the back window over his shoulder still pointing at my bike.

"Yep," I think to myself, "those bastards are going to come back tonight and try to take my bike." I was not overly worried since I was carrying a high capacity 9mm and was ready give them more than they have bargained for. Still, I did not relish spending a week or two in this place explaining to the law why I got into a shootout with two of their neighbors.

I decided not to unload the bike until I checked out the room. Things were getting sketchier by the minute, and I did not know what I was going to find on the other side of the door. For all I knew, there were more bad guys in the room waiting to rob me. I unzipped my pocket where I carry the 9mm and make sure I was ready to draw when I put the key in the door and gave it a turn. It was a simple pass key lock that a third grader could have kicked wide open in ballet shoes. The door swung open to reveal a single queen bed room configuration. The air was hot and stale inside. Clinton was probably president the last time this room saw a guest. I made sure no one was in the room, and having satisfied myself that I would not be jumped from the bathroom, I closed the door and opened the curtains so I could keep an eye on my bike while I checked out the room.

It takes me all of 10 seconds to realize I am not alone in the room. In fact, I am surrounded. There are ants on the floor, on the walls and the windows. Ants are no big deal when camping out, but I'll be damned if I make them suitemates in a motel room. I pulled back the bedspread and lifted the mattress to check for evidence of bedbugs. Sure enough, the little fellows had been there by the bushels.

This is where my own particular rules of the road came into play. My basic rule is, "Don't go looking for trouble, don't make trouble and if you find trouble, leave it behind." I had clearly made a mistake coming here. The place was not right and there was trouble on the horizon with the potential of me losing my bike that night and me being hurt or worse in the confrontation. I did what I should have done on the front end of the deal. I got the hell out of there. I had no desire to shoot two Indians over a bike and I sure did not want to get myself shot over a machine, so I threw my leg over the GS and donated my $37.50 to the motel owner who must surely have needed it worse than I did and I rode off toward Ruidoso. Unlike Carrizozo, Ruidoso is a nice resort town with a casino and a horse racing track, nice shops, hotels and restaurants. It was an hour away and I was bone-dead tired, but it was the right thing to do so on I rode.

***　　***　　***　　***　　***

If you have not noticed by the photographs by now, I will remind you that I am white. Being a white person means I rarely run into any kind of discrimination. Maybe people who do not like me or want to steal my bike, but outright discrimination is rare. So you can imagine my surprise when I encountered the desk attendant at the hotel in Ruidoso. I had gone online once I rode into town and found a hotel that said it was biker-friendly and looked like a nice clean place. This hotel had been remodeled in 2012, was multi-story and had rooms that one reached by means of interior hallways. These are almost always newer and cleaner and certainly safer than those old motels whose doors open out into the parking lot.

I parked the bike, took off my helmet and walked in wearing my yellow banana coat. There was a woman in front of me at the desk inquiring about the availability of a room. Since it was air-conditioned in the lobby, it was all good as far as I was concerned. I did not mind waiting. I was close enough to overhear her conversation with the desk clerk.

Woman traveler: "Do you have any rooms?"

Clerk: "Yes. We have plenty. What kind do you want?"

The woman traveler got her room. She, like the desk clerk, was Hispanic. Maybe they belonged to some secret order and had hand signals or something. All I know is she got her room in short order.

Now it was my turn.

Me: "I would like a room."

Clerk: "We don't have any."

This was not what I wanted to hear. My day had started over 12 hours earlier in Silver City, a town I was absolutely in love with and that had one really nice brewery. I had ridden through storms, been terrorized by slick oil signs and had avoided being in a gun battle with Indians to defend my bike, and now here I stood knowing I was being lied to. Shit was about to get real.

I let the clerk know in my nicest mediator/minister manner that I know there are rooms available and that any will do.

She looks at me coldly and tells me I cannot afford their rooms. I might not have been so mad, but I had parked my bike beside two Honda Goldwing motorcycles in their parking lot. If they were going to sell a room to a couple of Honda riders, they were damn sure going to give a BMW rider a room. I had all I was going to take from this little girl.

"Ma'am, there is nothing you have that I can't afford. You name any price you want and I'll pay it. I have the money to buy whatever you own so name your price and give me a room now."

I got my room. It cost all of $109.00. Now why she gave me grief I'll never know, but the race thing comes to mind. I took my gear and went upstairs and got cleaned up. Later that night after dinner, I walked around Ruidoso and found it to be a very nice place with inviting shops and galleries everywhere.

The next morning, I walked across the street to a new coffee house constructed to look like a ski lodge of the log cabin variety. It was one of the nicest coffee shops I have ever visited and friendly was the word.

Ruidoso like all of New Mexico is a great place. What went wrong between me and the hotel desk clerk the night before I'll never know. I can tell you it was instructive for me because on some level, and for just a few minutes, I got to feel like what a black person feels like when they encounter white bigotry and ignorance. It was no fun and it needs to stop. It is wrong on so many levels.

Silver City to Ruidoso had been a real adventure and now I was back in eastern New Mexico. Tomorrow I would pay a visit to a part of my childhood.

It was time to visit The Kid.

Chapter 14

Day Eight

"Little Green Men and a Six Gun"

-----Original Message-----
From: Brian House
Sent: Thursday, June 11, 2015 10:33 AM

Today was a really long, hot day. My eighth day in a row of riding. I put 375 miles on the GS today and I'm more than a little tired. I'm riding to Cloudcroft tomorrow where I'll set up my tent and rest in the cool air before riding down into southern Texas.

I left Ruidoso and headed to Roswell. Today would be my day to see the aliens and to explore the lore and myth of Billy the Kid. It was a beautiful morning with little to no wind. Just the kind of weather a flying saucer would no doubt prefer when landing in the middle of nowhere in New Mexico.

Roswell...was not what I expected. If you watch any sci-fi show, it will have you believe Roswell is just some little sleepy place of a few hundred people who have all, at one time or another, been abducted by aliens, laid out on an examining table and had their innards probed by some little green man. In reality, it is a town of 20 or so thousand folks with a whole lot of normal living going on, although even the normal businesses like hotels, restaurants and barbers are not above putting the little green man image on their billboards to help move sales along. McDonald's constructed their Roswell Restaurant and Playland in the shape of a flying saucer. Forgive me, I did not eat there.

I parked the GS on a side street having already cruised the main boulevard and determined where the aliens were to be found. There is a little section of main street that is "Alien Center." It reminds me of old Times Square in New York before it was cleaned up. There are numerous museums and institutes for the discovery and analysis of aliens and similar drivel. I went straight for the mother lode and hit the oldest Roswell U.F.O. Museum. It was the tallest, had the shiniest exterior (Aliens like shiny, right?) and most importantly, did not have any nut-jobs standing outside jabbering about what it must be like to REALLY meet an alien.

In I go to the UFO to scope out the con. It works like this: if you want to go beyond the velvet rope and behold room after room of alien narrative written and produced by people who have never laid eyes on one, then give the man your $10 and off you go. Or, if you are one of the unpersuaded who just wants a bumper sticker, then belly up to the control counter where your chest will be affixed with a UFO sticker that grants you admission only to the gift shop. I got such a sticker.

There is a special place in hell reserved for parents who let their kids run wild in stores. Little three-foot-tall monsters were running and screaming all over the gift shop. Could these be aliens at last? No, but almost. They were from Indiana. Their mother cared not one whit they were tearing the place apart. I made quick work of my bumper sticker quest and fled to the exit. Once outside on the sidewalk, I took a few minutes and walked down the street, but honestly, I couldn't work up enough energy and motivation to even take a picture of the place. It's just a little green man carnival sideshow and with so much that is truly beautiful and majestic in New Mexico, why would you waste another minute looking at six-foot-tall plastic green men? Which I did not. I got on my bike and weaved my way through some incredibly heavy traffic and made for Fort Sumner, the place of Billy the Kid's death and his purported last resting place.

The ride there lacked the fun of the high country twisties. It was more of a utilitarian, straight road, "let's get over there and visit The Kid" sort of ride. Fort Sumner is now a sleepy little town, the fort itself long gone with all that remains being a few foundational stones and a nice little picnic area. The Kid, however, is a multimillion-dollar enterprise. There are stores dedicated to The Kid, multiple museums, even multiple graves. Everyone wants a piece of The Kid.

I did my research ahead of time and knew which of the museums was recommended. It was the last and closest to the old fort, and it's really not much. Any of the little museums in Gatlinburg or Pigeon Forge will put The Kid's museums to shame. Cheap trinkets from China, a few t-shirt racks and bumper stickers and that's about it. Except for the grave which you can see in the accompanying photo. The Kid's grave. The final resting place of William Bonney or Henry McCarty or whoever he was. Some 21-year-old who let himself get used by powerful men in a war to enhance their wealth. Some of you who are reading this fought in one of those wars yourself a lifetime ago.

I'm an Old West buff. I know every street, alley and boardwalk in Tombstone. I've visited Ed Schefflin's grave and crawled in the abandoned mine works of Tombstone and Bisbee. I know way too much about Wyatt Earp and his crew and the men he really did kill. I have also spent way too much time reading about the Kid. Both men are famous, but there is a very important difference—the legend of Wyatt Earp can be proven. The Kid? Well, no one is even sure if he is in the ground. Pat Garrett was his good friend and Garrett would have the world believe he killed his friend in the dark and buried him quickly and his employers should have taken his word for it. That's not how it worked in those days. Many a dead outlaw was dug up and photographed, even if he was a might ripe, just so the good citizens would know he was dead and they could sleep better at night. Not so for The Kid. Everyone, including the provisional governor Lew Wallace (later to write Ben-Hur) was fine to take Garrett at his word.

So did I visit The Kid's grave? In my view of things, no. The Kid never died there. Garrett and his buddies helped The Kid ride off to Old Mexico where he lived out his life in anonymity and left the great state of New Mexico and Hollywood to get rich off the myth they made out of his name.

I started to leave the museum when I saw a woman running around a house off in the distance some three or 400 yards away. There was screaming. There was a small group of tourists looking that way. There was the museum clerk leaned into the window of a police cruiser talking to the deputy sheriff instead of taking my $1.50 at the cash register inside for a bumper sticker. The deputy burns rubber toward the running woman. A flip-flop wearing young man of a tourist brought me up to speed. Seems the screaming, running woman at the house and a man were having a domestic altercation, and she was screaming her head off for help while he was abusing her. The cashier called the law and now everyone was watching. Or trying to, the distance being too great for them to see. Everyone was really worried about the welfare of the women. The deputy was a woman. If only the tourists could see.

I went over to my tank bag and retrieved my 10-power monocular which I carry on trips. I walked backed to the group and started following the deputy's progress. She was doing fine and had matters well in hand. Flip-flop looks at my monocular and says, "Gee. You're making me look bad. Here you are on that bike and you're better prepared than we are." They were, in one of those deluxe Jeep Wranglers, pulling a trailer. Flip-flops continued, "We should be ready to help the deputy."

"Son," I said to myself, "you have no idea how ready I really am." But I kept quiet. The deputy got it squared away and I did not have to use my concealed carry license. I was on my way.

I got back to Alamogordo and was the most tired I've been on this trip. I could tell my reflexes were not very sharp, so I headed for a hotel. There were two men sitting outside keeping the Camel cigarette company in business. Both looked me up and down.

"How do you wear all that damn gear in this weather?" asked one of them.

"You get used to it," I replied

Which put me to thinking. Motorcycle riders are aliens to a lot of folks. We ride funny machines that intimidate people. We wear gear that makes us look like we walk on the moon. We ride solely for the joy of the ride.

Much of what is said about most of us bikers is not true. We are not thugs. We don't run drugs. We don't belong to gangs that engage in organized crime. We have jobs. Many of us have multiple college degrees. We have families. So, we're a lot like Billy the Kid. We are one thing, while people see what they want to see and make us out to be something entirely different.

My time in New Mexico is just about finished and then, like The Kid, I'll be moving on. First, I'm going to set up my tent and ride the high country one last time.

Ride safe and bless you all,
Brian

***　　　***　　　***　　　***　　　***

I was now into my second week of being on the road. I had ridden across the middle of America and so far had seen the deserts and the high country of both eastern and western New Mexico. My plan was to spend a few more days in the Land of Enchantment and then turn south to visit Big Bend National Park in far western Texas and stay a few nights in the ghost town of Terlingua down by the Mexican border. First though, I had to pay homage to those two icons of the New Mexican tourist industry—aliens and Billy the Kid. My eighth consecutive day on the bike was an effort to separate reality from the theatre of the mind. Since my arrival in New Mexico, I had been a sponge soaking up this culture of the southwest which is so much different from that of the hills of southeastern Kentucky. I was in America, but it was an alien land compared to where I lived in Kentucky. It was up to me to decide whether it was an acceptable place for a 50-something white guy on a German motorcycle. I found that it was.

It is a given about travel that the one who is traveling will be exposed to customs and peoples dissimilar to his own. Go to Africa or Asia and it is to be expected. Traveling across America the same thing happens and it demonstrates just how very different we Americans are from one another. That racial and ethnic diversity are two of the things I cherish most about America. We are many and one at the same time. It makes us a stronger, more resilient people who can draw upon the resources of many cultures when our country is stressed and under threat.

My little hometown of London has a population of somewhere around 10,000 people. It has been in existence in one form or another since 1825. London's big annual event is the World Chicken Festival. That event is mostly a carnival situated on the downtown streets replete with junk food and games for the kids, as well as numerous booths set up by various groups selling their wares. It ostensibly celebrates the life of Colonel Harlan Sanders, the founder of Kentucky Fried Chicken. He was no more a colonel than I am, which is to say we are both honorary Kentucky Colonels which, along with five dollars will get you the drink of your choice at Starbucks. The "Chicken Festival," as the locals call it, features the world's largest skillet and, as one might expect, the festival people fry the hell out of chickens during the event. That's about it for London's claim to fame. London is 96 percent white with Hispanics making up 0.47 percent of the population.

Alamogordo, New Mexico by contrast, is a town of approximately 36,000 with over 32 percent Hispanic residents. It is home to Holloman Air Force Base and has a large constituency of retired military living in the area. The German Air Force and other countries maintain a training presence there so their pilots can fly in the year-round good weather of the southwest. The Germans have built German language schools and churches for their itinerant training community and yet interact with the larger Alamogordo community as a whole. They host an annual Oktoberfest on base each year and invite the entire community. Beer and food is flown in from Germany for an authentic flavor to the event. Also in September is the annual Hot Air Balloon Festival that sees Alamogordo's skies filled with the colorful display of pilots flying their balloon aircraft all over the Tularosa Basin. There is fried chicken here, but the real culinary treat is the Hispanic food flavored by countless varieties of chilies. You can go mild or you can set your mouth on fire. The choice is yours.

I was enjoying the bilingual nature of every business and the presence of green chilies on everything at every meal. I just could not escape chilies. It is part of the people just like soup beans and corn bread are to southeastern Kentucky. Neither one is to be preferred over the other. They are just what people have. The same goes for race and language. We are all one people, but different at the same time and it makes America all the better. We can celebrate our differences and learn from one another, all the while embracing the things we treasure.

Treasure, I found, is also a local thing. In Kentucky, we treasure our racehorses and bourbon. I tend to treasure bourbon over horses, but that is just me. I can get kicked by either one, but I like to know when and how much of a kick is coming so I pour my own. Kentucky has Daniel Boone, Kit Carson and Muhammad Ali as some of its native sons. New Mexico has many favorite sons, but on this day of the ride I was focused on aliens and Billy the Kid.

I loaded up my bike at my Ruidoso hotel and checked out. Gone was the nasty desk clerk from the night before. She had been replaced by a thoroughly pleasant lady who directed me to a new coffee shop across the street. It was both a coffee shop and a wine store and had as its motto, "Dance As If No One Were Watching." Just the kind of vibe I needed after my encounter with last night's desk clerk. I downed two cups of expensive but thoroughly enjoyable coffee and a very hip multi-grain bagel, and then I was back on my bike and headed toward Roswell, the home of the alien invasion that maybe never happened.

Day Eight found me very beat up from riding the bike. I was so sore from the ill-fitting aftermarket seat that I rode standing up as much as possible. My bike, unlike Harley's and other cruiser types, is made for riding standing up and I found that I enjoyed standing on the pegs on straight stretches. Standing frequently alleviated the pain and made the ride bearable. I was generally tired from the ride and looking forward to a camping and reading day before I headed south into Texas, but first I was going to have a look at the little green men and then The Kid.

My experience with Roswell was framed entirely by television and movies. I had on my mind a dry, little dusty town, kind of like Mayberry from *The Andy Griffith Show* except with aliens. I assumed it would be a tiny main street with old buildings and maybe one police car. There would be the odd diner or two and a community gas station with an attendant who came out to fill up your tank all the while looking up to the sky to see if any more spaceships were about to land.

Suffice it to say, I was wrong. Roswell is a modern town with lots of streets and businesses everywhere. It has a population of around 50,000 and none of them look like aliens except those folks wearing alien suits and walking around downtown Main Street trying to get tourists to come into their alien shops.

Roswell became the UFO capital of America because of an alleged space ship crash that happened 75 miles from there in 1947. The debris was processed and stored by the local Roswell Army Air Field at the time. What it was has never been fully explained, but enterprising Americans being what they are, they saw a chance to make some money and the entire UFO industry was born. Indeed, the International UFO Museum is located in downtown Roswell. That museum was my destination.

Traffic was very heavy as I rode into downtown. I finally managed to find a place to park on a side street under a shade tree that afforded me some respite from the sun as I got off the bike and considered what to do with all my gear. It was well into the 90s by then and I had no way to safely secure my armored pants and coat and my helmet, so I decided to carry the helmet and wear the rest. I soon realized I would not be walking far or staying outside very long with all my gear on. I walked a few blocks to the museum and went in. As to whether it was a disappointment depends on what my expectations were going in, and since I had very, very low expectations, I was not disappointed. It was kitschy and goofy and just generally all the things that make stuff like an alien museum fun. The little kids that were in there were loving it, as were a few guys of the "plastic pen holder in my front shirt pocket" variety. There were, of course, no mounted and stuffed aliens and no verifiable documents, just a lot of things you can accept as fact if you are already one of the converted. I was not so I deferred from wasting an hour on a guided tour of nothing and walked into the souvenir shop to buy my alien sticker which would occupy a prominent spot on my luggage on the bike.

As I walked down the street, I encountered two college-age boys dressed in very hip, urban attire. That were drinking Slushies out of green plastic alien cups and having a blast. Further up the street, I walked past an elderly couple who were walking slow and gazing into all the alien store windows. He was wearing short pants and laced up wing tips with dark socks, while she was sensibly wearing a loose sleeveless dress. He had on some kind of veteran's ball cap that offered no protection for his neck, but did tell everyone he had protected us at some point. She was wearing a large straw hat that was doing the job hats should do. They too were having fun on this goofy little strip of real estate.

I thought to myself, "This is great. Here are people having fun soaking it all in, knowing none of this can ever be proven. It's like being on the inside of a joke that is being played on us. We all go along with it and it's fun."

I walked back to the bike and put my stickers on my aluminum luggage and sat for a few minutes under the tree, sipping water through my CamelBak tube and being very glad I had it. This was already a hot day and it was going to be a lot hotter when I pulled out from under the tree. It would take me over two hours of hot riding to cover the 90 miles from Roswell to Fort Sumner where I would finally have my encounter with the legend and lore that has become Billy the Kid.

I rode down Roswell's alien Main Street passing little inflatable green men in front of businesses and the local McDonald's which was built to look like a flying saucer, though the burgers would be the same. Main Street gave way to Highway 285. It was busier than I liked for a fun day of riding, but my turnoff onto Fort Sumner Road came after about 40 miles. After that, I was on the isolated two-lane road for 50 miles and by myself for the most part. I saw only a few cars during those 50 miles of rough asphalt riding past ranch land that appeared largely unchanged since ranchers put cattle here hundreds of years ago. This was the same range that The Kid and his "Pals," as he called them, rode during the Lincoln County War.

The road was practically deserted, so I set my bike's cruise control and stood up with my visor raised and let the cool air blow over me. I thought of The Kid riding around here and what a different life that was. He was only 21 when he was allegedly killed by his friend Sheriff Pat Garrett who would himself be murdered some years later. The land is settled now and towns and aliens and air force bases and green chilies are all part of the place, but none occupy a space as prominent as Billy the Kid.

The Kid is everywhere in southeastern New Mexico. Signs of him are ubiquitous. There are countless t-shirt designs of The Kid as there have been 25 movies made about The Kid. Movies stars clamored to play The Kid. Audie Murphy, Paul Newman, Kris Kristofferson, Emilio Estevez, Val Kilmer and Donnie Wahlberg all took their turn trying to bring The Kid to life on the silver screen. Musicians sing about him and composers like Aaron Copeland have composed musical scores around the myth of The Kid.

On a much smaller scale are the gift shops and the roadside booths that do their bit to cash in on The Kid. Year after year, carloads of tourists make the journey to Fort Sumner and Lincoln, New Mexico to draw close to The Kid, and yet it is no understatement to say that no one has much of an idea who The Kid really was.

Only one verifiable photograph of The Kid exists. It is as famous in these parts as the Mona Lisa is in others, but it is much more hotly debated over what it does and does not reveal about The Kid. He stands in the photograph wearing a hat that is crumpled and cocked to one side. He is holding a rifle and wearing a six gun. His teeth are crooked and he perhaps has a prominent overbite. He certainly is not wealthy.

It is generally agreed The Kid was born Henry McCarty and was later known as William H. Bonney. He killed men with a gun. Some records put the number as high as 21, others say it was "only eight." Take your pick on the number, but The Kid was a killer. The how's and the why's of all that killing are a matter of perspective. Some say The Kid was just an outlaw. Others attribute to him nobler inclinations saying he fought on the side of justice during the Lincoln County War, which was a business dispute over dry goods and cattle sales in Lincoln County, New Mexico in the spring of 1878. The Kid got himself and some of his friends tangled up in the fight. People died and The Kid came out on the short end of the stick and had to flee for his life. Now, depending upon whom you believe, The Kid was either murdered by his good friend Pat Garrett on July 15, 1881 at Fort Sumner or Garrett let him escape into the night to old Mexico where The Kid lived out his days in anonymity. Local folks have profitably embraced the notion The Kid is buried at Fort Sumner or nearby and have set about making a living selling admission to The Kid's grave. The Kid would get a laugh out of the fact he has two graves in the area as competing businesses are trying to cash in on his bones. I chose the site generally recognized as the one most likely to be The Kid's grave if ever he was buried there.

I paid my money and walked around back of the little building that was the Billy the Kid Museum and took a look at his grave. It was just a tombstone surrounded by a wrought iron fence that was doing a good job of preventing anyone from stealing the stone which had apparently been a problem in the past. Pat Garrett said it was The Kid. Some others said it was The Kid, but no one took a picture of the Kid lying in death repose. Posterity was left with taking the word of The Kid's good friend that he was in the ground. I doubt it, but who am I to interfere with what has become a multimillion-dollar enterprise for so many? I bought my Billy the Kid sticker for my bike and, having contributed to the local economy, went out to my bike.

As I was putting the sticker on the bike, I heard someone screaming from a house across the road. I stood there and watched as the thing unfolded. It was a violent domestic dispute between a man and a woman. The police had already been called by the time I realized what was going on. Other tourists were watching from the parking lot of the museum. No one seemed to be willing to offer any help and who could blame them since they were all there with wives and children or were too old to help. I watched the police officer get matters quickly under control and then I was on my way. What would I have done if the officer had been attacked? Who knows and I am glad I did not have to find out. I really did not want to make the call home telling Susan her preacher husband had been in a gun fight at Billy the Kid's grave.

So I had seen them both. I had been to the holy ground of aliens and The Kid. I had visited museums and gift shops and more importantly, ridden and walked on the ground where these things happened. My thoughts drifted more to The Kid than to the aliens.

The Kid was only 21 when he died or rode off into obscurity. He never made a dime off his name other than to steal some food and a few dollars here and there. He was poor coming into this world and poor going out, and yet millions upon millions of dollars have been made off of his name. A man who kills eight men or 21 men is no saint, so perhaps it is a certain kind of justice that he never profited from all that killing while others have. It is hard to understand his life, but altogether easy to appreciate the enterprising nature of the people of this area who saw a way to make a living and did so. They took the story of a petty thief and murderer and turned it into a grand American romance and opera that continues to this day. That others could seize upon rumors of a spaceship crash and launch a similar enterprise just goes to show you that there is always a way to make a living in the desert if you try hard enough.

It had been a long day on the bike for me. I decided to return to Alamogordo for the night and then ride up into the mountains at Cloudcroft and camp for a few days in the cool mountain air. I needed a break from the heat of the desert.

The solitude of the trip had become for me almost monastic in nature. I went hours without talking to anyone. What conversations I did have were usually informational with me asking or answering questions or doing business at stores and restaurants. I had wanted time to think and now I had it. Traveling alone afforded me the opportunity to become an observer. I watched life all around me. I listened to the plain and ordinary conversations of people living their ordinary lives. I would catch a snippet of a phone conversation here and then a phrase or two of a sidewalk chat there as I moved about. I wondered why people would intentionally come out into the blazing sun wearing only short pants and a tank top. Why do people put green chilies on fried eggs? Why does someone run a cash register at the Billy the Kid Museum or work day after day as a tour guide at the International UFO Museum? Who was the rancher standing at his gate as I rode by on the Fort Sumner Road? I'll never talk to him and yet he is a part of my trip, a piece of the mosaic of the experience that became my ride to recovery, my celebration of life. Maybe he was a cancer survivor like me or maybe he was as healthy as a horse and would never be sick a day in his life and would die someday in his sleep at 98. Who was the girl who served me my coffee and bagel all the way back in Ruidoso? Will she be there when I return next year or will her life have carried onto some other place? Did the desk clerk from the night before learn her lesson or is she going to repeat her behavior tonight?

Who knows? All those unanswered questions are just part of the amazing and delightful journey that is life. I do not need to know all the answers. It is enough for me to make the journey, to drink deep from the well of life and embrace it for all of its wonderful uncertainty and accept the bizarre and illogical along with the things that are ordered and sensible. It is life and it is beautiful and wonderful and it never gets dull. Breathe it in for as long as you can.

Chapter 15

Day Nine

A New Direction

-----Original Message-----

From: Brian House

Sent: Friday, June 12, 2015 12:38 AM

Tonight I was supposed to be camping in Cloudcroft and I almost made it. As things stand, I am writing this installment at a "lay your head down" motel in Seymour, Texas, some 420 miles from what I had hoped would be my camping spot for the night. But things change.

My day began at 6:00 a.m. at the Hampton Inn, Alamogordo. I decided to write my blog in the morning since I had been really tired the night before. I knew what I wanted to write so my plan was to brew coffee in the little in-room brewer and get started. I would then go downstairs to the lobby and refuel on the Hampton's better grade of coffee. So, I opened up the brewer and...bugs crawled out.

I started looking around the desk and the wall and there were dozens and dozens of bugs. They were everywhere! Not bedbugs, just some kind of bug about a half-inch long that looked like a lightning bug without the lights. I went down for coffee and came back and wrote the blog while fighting off the attack of the legions of bugs at the same time. Once the blog posted, I then began loading so I could get out and head to Cloudcroft for camping and breakfast.

While I was loading, the manager on duty came out to smoke. I told him about the bugs and he immediately went in to get pest control on the problem. By the time I was loaded, the head manager spoke with me, apologized and comped me the room. I was satisfied and rode onto Cloudcroft.

I followed my policy of giving every restaurant a second chance and this morning at Cloudcroft I gave that second chance to Dave's, and Dave's was on its game. I had the day's special—biscuits and gravy with sausage crumbled on top, thick sliced bacon and two scrambled eggs and coffee. It was excellent. The owner offered to charge my phone for me when he saw me checking my battery and my waitress brought me several packets of crackers for my camping at no charge. I'll be back at Dave's this fall when Susan and I come out to visit my son. Which brings me to my change of plans:

I had selected my camping spot at the Silver River campground outside Cloudcroft and was in the process of unloading my bike when Elliott called. The Air Force had just notified him he would be sworn in and commissioned as a First Lieutenant next Tuesday morning in Nashville and he wanted to know if I could make it back in time to see him sworn in. I told him I would make some calculations and call him back. Well, there went the camping plans. I checked my maps, made a plan, called Elliott and told him I was on my way and got on the bike and headed for home. Tonight, I'm here in little Seymour 1,019 miles from London. I'll get home in time to pack and turn around and drive to Nashville. I wouldn't miss his swearing in for the world.

I encountered a lot of West Texas wind today, and it was bad, real bad. One good decision I think I made before starting out on my trip was to remove the top box. I think if I had it on the bike it would have been near impossible to control. Also, last night I decided to remove the visor/mud deflector from my helmet. It is much, much quieter and my head is more stable in the wind.

I took the bypass around Lubbock today and it was a congested, misdirected, confusing rider's nightmare with construction zones everywhere. Texas is just so big that places like Lubbock don't look significant on a map and yet they are true cities.

Did I tell you that the great state of Texas oils its roads? Well, Texas didn't tell me. They just let me come around a curve at 75 mph and wham; there is fresh oil on the road! I'll give the Texans this: they do things completely or not at all. Not only did they pour fresh oil all over the road, they then spread gravel on top of the oil "to make it safer." In whose world is such a mess safe? As it was, I kept the bike upright and let the GS find its way through the stuff. That mess went on for hours all afternoon.

Texas has beautiful rest areas. It's kind of a private club because they don't have any signs telling you they are there. You just sort of see them as you swoosh on by and watch the locals go to their own private Texas potty. So considerate of them.

When you are looking at a Texas map, you need a Texas frame of mind. Get rid of your Kentucky easterner thinking. All those little roads on the map that seem to lead to out of the way towns you've never heard of? They're actually four-lane roads with divided medians, speed limits of 75 mph and they go through towns that have less than 500 people. One town after another offering no services of any kind. For hundreds of miles. For hours and hours.

General Motors and the other auto makers have secretly developed cars and trucks that get over 200 miles to the gallon. You and I don't have these vehicles, but everyone in Texas does because there are no gas stations in most small communities. The only way these ranchers and townsfolk can survive, in my view, is to have the top secret, high mileage cars of tomorrow right now.

I rode through the Llano Estacado today, the Staked Plains of west Texas. It is flat and beautiful and oh so very, very big. I don't know how a handful of Texas Rangers ever brought law and order to the place. Had the buffalo not been exterminated, I think the Comanche might still be out there today. The vastness of the American West is so special. The punishing wind, the lack of gas, goofy "oil the road and don't tell anyone road" policies—none of that matters. This part of America is so beautiful it just has to be seen. I know this: I'll be back and I can't wait for the next trip.

Tomorrow I will ride into Arkansas. Let's see how far I can get as I make the journey to be with Elliott as he takes his oath and prepares to serve at Holloman AFB, Alamogordo, NM.

Be safe and bless you all,
Brian

***　　　***　　　***　　　***　　　***

Day Nine was to have been the beginning of a two-day layover in the high mountains. I had previously scouted out the area earlier in the trip and had a pretty good idea where I would pitch my tent and set up camp. I would be a few miles outside Cloudcroft at an elevation of about 9,000 feet. I would have cool nights which make for great sleeping and warm days, but not unbearably hot like at the lower elevations. I would store what little freeze dried food I had brought up in a tree and shower at the campground shower facilities which were discreetly tucked away on a short path.

I had packed a lot of gear for this precious part of the trip. I had tested several tents and sleeping bags before deciding which ones would go in the waterproof duffle bag I carried strapped down on the back seat of the bike. I had a lightweight collapsible portable camp chair, cook stove, fuel, hatchet, rope, mess kit, detergents, towels, small broom and dust pan, bug sprays, books and journals among other things. It all added up to a considerable amount of gear and weight, but I was planning on using it at Cloudcroft and then later down at Big Bend National Park while on my southwest Texas swing. But, things change and they changed for me in a big way on Day Nine.

The Day Eight ride from Ruidoso to Roswell and Fort Sumner had exhausted me, so I returned to the Hampton Inn in Alamogordo and spent the night in a clean room. I enjoyed the added bonus of being right next door to a couple of chain restaurants with ice cold beer and lots of widescreen TVs so I could get my baseball fix. I got up the morning of Day Nine at 6:00 a.m. so I could write my blog covering Day Eight's events. I decided to make coffee in the in-room brewer. When I opened the brewer to pour water into the brew tank, bugs came running out of the tank. I started looking around the brewer which led me to inspect the wall unit air conditioner. There were dozens upon dozens of bugs crawling out of the AC unit and resting on the wall around the unit. Needless to say, I took a pass on the in-room coffee and made my way down to get coffee in the lobby. I returned and wrote my blog while fighting the onslaught of the room bugs. They were not bedbugs, just some sort of harmless seasonal infestation that apparently happens sometimes in the southwest. It was no big deal except that the room was well over $100 for the night, and for that price I sure did not expect to have an army of bugs bunking with me.

The good news is that, like most things on the trip, it all worked out because I rolled with it. I finished my blog, packed my gear and took it downstairs to load. As I was loading, I had the opportunity to speak with one of the managers on duty who had come outside for his smoke break. I mentioned the bug thing to him and he immediately went inside to investigate. I continued loading and by the time I went to the front desk they had investigated and verified my report and comped my room. I was fine with the whole thing and left knowing I would stay there again.

I caught perfect weather for my early morning ride up to Cloudcroft. Cool breeze and bright blue skies abounded. I decided to give Dave's Restaurant in Cloudcroft another chance, and this time I was greeted with excellent food and a super friendly wait staff. I think I must have looked very much like the road weary traveler I had become. They brought me extra-large portions of bacon along with my biscuits and gravy, recharged my phone and gave me lots of crackers in packets so I could have them for my camp meals. All at no extra charge. I finished my meal and walked around town for a little while, eventually stopping in the High Altitude Outfitters store located just down the street from Dave's. The owner was on duty and willingly entertained my questions about where to camp. This was not the first time he had been asked the "where should I camp" question. He responded with a few of his own, designed to determine whether I would be backpacking, using an RV or something in between. When I told him I was riding a motorcycle and traveling with packed gear, he made several recommendations. When I told him I wanted a secluded spot that was accessible with a touring bike like mine where I could sleep with the bike beside me, he knew the spot. I left there with some good information as well as several shirts and the always necessary stickers for my bike.

I rode out of town and made the short ride of a mile or so to the Silver River campground that my new friend at High Altitude had recommended. I slowed down and began winding my way into the campground along the narrow paved roads that curve through most national forest campgrounds and are designed to keep speeds slow and afford pockets of privacy. I stopped for a minute at the camp host's trailer to check in. He told me to take my pick of any spot since I would be the only camper who had checked in today.

I wanted a spot that would give me a vista of a view looking out over the lower elevations, and I wanted privacy and, if it was not too much to ask, one that would be reasonably close to the restrooms, but not right next door since I did not want to hear slamming doors all night. I found one that looked like it would do, but upon closer inspection the tent sight was too rocky. I tried another, but it was too steep. Finally, on the third try I found the spot that would be my nirvana for the next two days. The tent site was level and smooth and the picnic table looked out onto a view of open mountains for miles. This was it. Here I would rest and restore my inner self, not to mention rest my very sore backside. I would read some and write in my journal and perhaps enjoy a wee bit of bourbon should the moment arise. No bears were active in the area, so I was likely to not have to kill anything in camp. Camp hosts frown upon people who blow holes through campground bear. I was ready to finally get some rest.

The first order of camp for me is always setting up my tent. I learned this the hard way years ago as a boy on camping trips. Youthful enthusiasm being what it is, I would bring my gear into camp, throw it on the ground with the other boys and then go off exploring or fishing, only to return at dark and spend a miserable hour or two stumbling around over tent pegs and guide lines trying to put up my tent in the rain. By then my gear would be soaked and the mood of the experience would have dimmed considerably. This is, of course, where boys learn to curse. Or rather, where they first feel emboldened enough to use the same words they heard their fathers use before in fits of frustration. Now properly motivated, the boys can curse and do so with full gusto for their words now have meaning and they will always have this meaning from this day forward because they know what cursing means and what it is for.

The problem with good cursing is it conflicts with being a preacher. At least it conflicts with what most people think a preacher should be. I am, as you can tell by this point in the book, not that kind of preacher. I'll curse if the occasion and misery warrant, but given ordinary circumstances I'll also do my best to seek other means of communication and self-expression. Part of that means I will do my best to plan ahead and put up the damn tent.

I was in the process of unloading my tent when my cell phone rang. How it rang up there I really do not know because I should have been well away from a signal, but ring it did. I could tell by the particular ring that it was my son calling. Elliott's voice was light and cheerful, which was a good thing when receiving an unexpected call so far from home. The Air Force, THE United States Air Force, had called after months of Elliott waiting and informed him he would be sworn in as a First Lieutenant in four days in Nashville. Elliott wanted me to be there if I wanted to be there and if I thought I could make it.

I was only 1,500 miles from home and had no return route planned for a direct return. I was beat up and had saddle sores so bad I wanted to shoot that damned aftermarket saddle. My neck was sore from wind pushing my head around. I would have to average 500 miles a day with no break to do it while navigating on the fly.

There was no way I was going to miss his swearing in. I could get there. I would get there. He could take it to the bank. I studied my maps for a few minutes and decided I could make it by riding due west to Artesia, New Mexico and then across west Texas through some pretty barren land. I would have to hit the interstates some in Texas and Arkansas, but the majority of the return ride would still be on backroads. I could do this, but I had not a moment to lose.

What I did lose was my southern swing through west Texas. Big Bend National Park, Terlingua, Marfa and Alpine would all have to wait for my next trip. My son needed me and I was going to be there if I had to ride up to the swearing in wearing my banana outfit and smelling like roadkill.

I called Elliott back and told him I would see him in Nashville, and I hung up the phone and restrapped my duffle bag. I had not even unzipped it so soon did the call come after I picked my camping spot.

I decided to leave immediately and ride to Artesia and see how I was doing. It was about 11:00 a.m., so I had a lot of daylight left since it was mid-June. I could cover a lot of ground. I would have to plan my route in general and then specifically in stages as I rode. I would use refueling stops to consult my maps and make detailed route decisions throughout the day. I would rely on Payday candy bars and water to get me through the day and I would ride until I could ride no more.

The ride down the mountain from Cloudcroft was exhilarating as I carved through one curve after another. I worked hard to resist the temptation to really turn the throttle and try to make fast time. I was too far from home and too unfamiliar with the roads to do anything other than ride at a reasonable pace and trust long hours in the saddle to get the job done.

I set my sets on Artesia, New Mexico some 95 miles and over two hours away. I arrived to find a very quaint little town. Artesia is a community of about 12,000 people. It sits in the heart of the oil rich Permian Basin. You can call it an oil and gas town and be right on the money. The first commercial oil well in New Mexico was drilled just east of Artesia in 1924 by the Yates family. The Yates chose to live and raise their family in Artesia, and they exhibited a keen and sustaining interest in improving reading and the arts. The public library is a work of art in itself with murals adorning its walls. Over the years, impressive bronze statues have been commissioned to portray significant people and events of this part of New Mexico. I rode by these statues as I made my way east. Artesia, I could see even from the seat of the GS, is a town worth visiting to walk the tree-lined main street, take in the art and eat at one of the several restaurants and a brew pub doing brisk business downtown. I made a mental note to visit this special place upon my return to New Mexico.

My ride from the west of Artesia had been unremarkable, but I could not say the same for the ride on the east side of Artesia toward Lovington, NM. I soon came upon the oil production fields. Some seemed to be oil wells, others were gas wells and possibly others were fracking stations. There were thousands upon thousands of these wells as far as the eye could see on either side of the road to the horizon. Even to my unsophisticated eye, it was obvious the principal economic engines here were oil and gas production and ranching. Those thousands of wells translate into billions of dollars of revenue poured back into the economy, but, just like strip mines in southeastern Kentucky, they are not pretty. I have never considered myself a judge of what other people do in their house so I pass no judgment on what I saw that day, but I will say I do not want to make those oil fields a view I would see from the front porch of my house any more than I would want to see the raw, stripped-mined, flat-topped mountains back in Kentucky.

Lovington marked the end of the really big oil production fields at least from the road, although I knew there were plenty more out there. My plan was to ride on Highway 82 from Lovington up to Lubbock, Texas where I would take the bypass around the city and continue on 82 all the way across Texas, riding well north of metropolitan Dallas, and entering Arkansas at Texarkana.

The wind was waiting for me in west Texas. I had suspected it would be there so I removed the visor from my helmet before starting out for the day. The visor, I had found, served as a kind of sail in heavy wind and would cause my head to be snapped to and fro as I fought to keep the bike on track. A day of that sort of head yanking made for a really sore neck, so I sought to avoid that punishment on the return trip by canning the visor. The wind was still terrible, but my head remained more stable than before which meant I would not fatigue as quickly and should be able to get more hours in the saddle.

Much of west Texas is open country. It gives the appearance of being unsettled, but it has long since been converted into ranches and farms. Small communities dot west Texas and each has its own identity. Lubbock serves as the metropolitan hub for the area along Highway 82. The Lubbock metropolitan area has a population of around 300,000, so it is a good-sized city. At rush hour, it is even worse. Riding a motorcycle at rush hour on a congested interstate bypass undergoing construction and having numerous detours made it a nightmare. Still, I took my time and after a few stops at gas stations and one elementary school parking lot, I figured out where I was and where I needed to go and I eventually made it around the city.

The problem, if you want to call it that, with impromptu travel is the open-ended nature of each day. I knew I needed to get home and I knew where home was. I generally knew how I was going to get there but not specifically. Those lack of specifics are where the little problems are found.

I made it to the east side of Lubbock by 6:00 p.m. There were countless hotels at every exit as I rode along, but I wanted to use as much daylight as possible and the sun was still high in the sky. There are always hotels about every 30 miles in Kentucky and Tennessee so I figured it would be the same as I left Lubbock.

Rule #1 when in Texas—Never forget Texas is big. Really big.

Idalou, Texas: Too soon. I'll ride on. Lots of daylight left.

Lorenzo, Texas: I knew a golf pro named Lorenzo once. He could not play golf worth a damn. I rode on.

Ralls, Texas: Still lots of daylight. Nice little town, but I'll ride on.

Crosbyton, Texas: Sun is starting to set, but I can still make some good time. I'll ride on.

Dickens, Texas: Where did the sun go? It's getting dark and I cannot find a motel anywhere. In fact, I am going to need gas soon and I have not seen a gas station in hours.

Guthrie, Texas: There is a sign for it, but it is nowhere to be seen. Almost pitch dark now.

Benjamin, Texas: I was at a critical juncture now. My gas was almost to the "E". I was not going to run out of gas because I was carrying two spare gallons in reserve canisters. Still, if I could not find gas I would no doubt not find a hotel, so I might just be spending the night sleeping by my bike on the side of the road in the bushes. Not a bad thing, but not a sign of good planning either. I approached Benjamin at a slow pace prepared to make a quick turn if I ever saw the town proper, which I never did. What I did see was a tiny gas station on the left side of the road. It was a small, very small convenience store-type affair with two pumps out front. It was the first gas station I had seen in hours and it was now dark. I pulled up to the pump and got off the bike. There was a small wooden bench set against the brick wall of the store by the front door. Two young women in their early 20s were seated there. They both had urban aspirations given the number of tattoos and body piercings adorning their bodies. It being summer and the young ladies wearing cutoff jeans and tank tops and little else, lots of tattoos and piercings were visible. I asked them if there was a hotel in town. The older of the two girls replied:

"Not here, but there is a pretty good one on down the road in

Seymour. I use it all the time."

Hmmm...local girl uses motel "all the time." What kind of recommendation was that and what did I look like? Obviously she did not appreciate me for the ordained clergy of a liberal left-leaning denomination that I was. Still, I now had gas and I needed a room so that was good enough. I thanked the girls, paid for my gas and rode to Seymour. I would get there, pay for a room and go to a restaurant for dinner. All would be well.

My ride to Seymour broke one of my rules of the road when traveling solo—do not ride after dark. Riding a motorcycle is an inherently dangerous activity just as is driving a car at 80 mph, but the cultural perspective is different. Riding a motorcycle in rural deer country by yourself after dark is just plain always dangerous and now I was doing it. I was riding in the dark on a rural road because I had made a promise and because I had played my hunches and guesses and hopes about what I might find on the road all the way out to the setting of the sun and now I had no more daylight. Let me hit a deer out here or an oil slick and run off the road and I would be royally, truly screwed. I have always been a cautious but never fearful rider and this trip made me, I am convinced, a much better rider. Still, bad judgment is bad judgment, and I owned up to it in my mind and soldiered on being hyper vigilant for deer and any other road surprises.

I saw the little motel on the left as I reached the outskirts of Seymour. It was an old road motel born of the post-World War II automobile travel boom. It had a courtyard and what at one time had been a small playground for children. The door of each room opened to the outside. The motel office had lights on and the neon red "Vacancy" sign was illuminated. It was almost nine o'clock and rooms were available. I could see several late model, heavy duty pick-up trucks parked in front of rooms, so I figured this was a place where construction crews usually stayed long-term. It would be safe and should be reasonably clean.

I entered the tiny lobby and was struck by how clean it was. The small room was decorated in Hindu motif with various Hindu gods and holy shrines of that faith depicted in paintings hanging on the pastel blue walls. Tiny statues of Hindu gods were situated around the room on shelves and the motel counter. I could hear a television playing quietly in the living quarters that were behind the front desk. I rang the little bell on the counter and waited. The last time I did this in Carrizozo things had not worked out so well.

In a moment, the beaded curtain stirred and an older lady dressed in traditional Hindu attire came out and greeted me. She was pleasant and smiled at me. I paid for a room and began to fill out the registration card. My hands were shaking so badly from gripping the handlebar all day that I could barely write. My hostess was very polite and concerned:

"You are exhausted. Take some breakfast cereal and eat it before you go to bed." She pointed to two clear plastic cereal dispensers located on what was the breakfast table in the lobby. One cereal appeared to be off-brand Fruit Loops and the other a Raisin Bran of some sort.

I appreciated her kindness, but declined and went to my room got out of my gear and unpacked. I then walked outside and heard two of the construction guys talking to each other. They had sent their buddy to the nearest fast food place which was some ways away to get their food. Unless I wanted to gear back up and ride some more in the dark, I would have to make do with what I had in my pack.

I had two choices. I could break out the camping gear, fire up my stove and cook some freeze dried backpacking meal, or I could rummage through my tank bag and eat what I could find. I was too tired to get the stove out, so I dove into my luggage to eat what I could find without cooking.

It came down to a bottle of warm Sprite, a can of Vienna sausages with a temperature of about 90 degrees, the crackers the waitress gave me at Dave's in Cloudcroft and two airline-sized bottles of vodka, which I of course was carrying for purely medicinal purposes. The little motel did have an ice machine so I filled the tiny plastic thing that passes for an ice bucket and sat down to enjoy my road meal. I was about halfway through the can of sausages when I broke out laughing. I have friends and family who fancy themselves luxury travelers and they would never be caught dead eating like this. They have no idea what they are missing. If I had eaten at a really nice restaurant that night in Seymour, I would not have the memories of my Vienna sausage, crackers and vodka meal.

I had ridden another demanding day on the bike. Long hours, heavy winds and indifferent food had been the order of my day. It was a priceless experience. I had answered the call to be there for my son and I had undertaken a long journey to be there. It was something I had to do by myself. No one could help me now. I was well and truly on my own and I was doing it even when navigating through uncharted territory. With every turn of the wheels of my bike, I was alive and purposed in my living. I was carrying on. What cancer had tried to take from me I had retained. I was still out there, still being who I was and staying in the fight.

Memorable days come along and this one ranks right there at the top. My destination lay a thousand miles east of me. I would ride my way there and I would do it for my son, for life and for all the good days that remain to be embraced.

Chapter 16

Day 10

Change on the Horizon

-----Original Message-----
From: Brian House
Sent: Saturday, June 13, 2015 12:19 AM

The picture of my bike is what it looks like 10 hours into a 12.5-hour ride day. The GS looks none the worse for wear, but I certainly do. I covered 595 miles today and regrettably about 200 of it was interstate, and during Little Rock rush hour as well! You would think such a long day in the saddle would leave little time for meeting people along the way, but actually it was one of my more memorable days on this trip.

I left Seymour, Texas at 7:15 this morning. The skies looked like rain was possible, but none came. When I went out to load my bike, the parking lot of the motel was alive with the activity of work crews loading their trucks for the day's work. All were young men except for one middle-aged fellow who was clearly the foreman. We were all busy to be somewhere else, so no small talk. Just men getting ready to go. I was away and gone before they left. As I rode through Texas, I passed by who knows how many hundreds of thousands of acres of rangeland. I saw very few cattle and more than a few ranches for sale. I never did see anyone working cattle, although I did see a few stock trailers being hauled around by pickup trucks. These appeared to be horse haulers. What I did see in abundance were oil wells and fracking sites galore. When I drove through Artesia, NM yesterday, I came upon an oil field that went on for at least 10 miles with the pump stations stretching to the horizon.

So, where are the cowboys? My strong suspicion is they work for much better pay for these fracking companies. The workers' trucks parked at the motel had the name of a "ranch" painted on each door. I looked in the beds of the trucks and did not see livestock tools. What I did see was a lot of equipment to work on other equipment and all of it emitted the smell of grease and oil. Fracking has become a real flashpoint topic in the west and those who oppose it have become militant in their opposition. I suspect the fracking company uses the word "ranch" in its public name in order to protect their workers from some anti-fracking zealot. Those who used to be cowboys now work upon the same ranch, but it's a different enterprise altogether.

"Maybe there just aren't any cowboys left anymore," I thought as I rode. Around mid-afternoon I stopped at Texarkana, Texas to get a soft drink. A UPS truck pulled into the gas station and parked beside me. In a few moments, the truck's door slid open and there stood Hoss Cartwright's doppelganger, or at least an east Texas two-thirds-scale version with a mustache and wearing brown short pants. Turns out he was really into Enduro riding and Honda bikes. So, we did what I have done so many times on this trip—have one of those totally unexpected but very fun and entertaining conversations between strangers about a shared interest.

Mini-Hoss, as I call him, was passionate about the new Honda Africa Twin motorcycle that is supposed to be the GS killer. I told Mini-Hoss I was very interested in the Twin, but I was happy with my GS. He wanted to know if I did the valve work on the GS myself. I told him "No" and that I lacked the tools and the expertise to undertake such a project. He nodded his Hoss-head in agreement and then out of nowhere he said:

Hoss: "You ride a lot of miles?"
Me: "Well, I am on this trip."

Hoss: "You ever get the old ass-ache? All of us Enduro guys get it. You get it? You get ass-ache on that BMW?"

There are times when the truth hurts and then there are times like today when hurting is the truth. "Yes. On this trip I sure have from all the miles."

Hoss, smiling as he heads inside the gas station carrying a box to deliver: "Well, that's something you and me got in common. We both got ass-ache."

And people think traveling solo is a silent undertaking.

I stopped in Jonesboro, Arkansas for the night and went to an Applebee's that was adjacent to the hotel. I sat at the bar and had a salad and a beer while watching the Cardinals and the Royals play. I was about halfway through my salad when four guys came in wearing their work clothes. They had been in the sun all day and had the dirt on their clothes to give evidence of hard work done. Turns out they were large crane operators and they were from Kentucky. I was wearing a UK shirt and that got us started talking. When I told them I was a lawyer (don't blame me; they asked and I wasn't about to lie) it almost killed the conversation, but as soon as I told them I was on a motorcycle trip, the entire conversation became one of each of us sharing with the others where our journeys have taken us recently. We passed the time there as fellow travelers, defined not by our occupations, but by our desire to go and see and do things that take us away from the familiar comforts of home. I left the boys there while they were eating stacks of hot wings, their version of a late night meal. It felt good to have spent those minutes talking with them just as I had done with the Brits a few days earlier.

Tomorrow I will be back in Kentucky and may make it home if the weather and I hold out. As I ride, I'm sure I'll be thinking of Mini-Hoss and the crane operators. That is, until I meet the next interesting person on the road tomorrow.

Be safe and bless you all,
Brian

***   ***   ***   ***   ***

Day 10 was long hours and lots of miles—12.5 hours and almost 600 miles by the time my day ended. Solo riding being such a solitary endeavor, I had plenty of time to think and absorb everything that came my way.

The whole fracking thing continued to intrigue me. When I realized the pick-up trucks at the motel were frackers, even though the trucks had "ranch" painted on the side, I began to understand this was a volatile issue that might hold more than a little degree of physical risk for the employees of fracking companies.

You cannot blame the men and women who are working on the fracking crews. They are just taking the best job out there and doing the best they can to provide for their families. They would still be riding horses and working cattle if the pay was better, but beef prices never seem to make that happen. Still, there is no denying the land looked scarred from horizon to horizon and the air smelled less than pristine. I got online and read about the water quality and pollution issues that environmentalists were raising relative to the fracking process. The spokespeople for the fracking companies all had marvelous academic pedigrees and opinions to refute these health and quality of life issues, and they had millions of dollars behind them to get their message out that fracking was safe and no lasting harm would come from this extraction process. The day before, I met a pickup truck on the road as I rode into Texas. It was an older model coated with lots of red dirt and more than a few dents and scratches on the red and white body. It was being driven by what I took to be an older rancher. He was wearing a straw western style hat and a blue-checkered long sleeve, collared ranch shirt. He had erected a four-by-eight-foot plywood sign in the bed of his truck that said, "Say Hell No To The Frackers." There was no doubt where he stood on the issue.

I get both sides of the fracking issue. Grow up in the coalfields of eastern Kentucky and you have the whole mining versus the environment thing in your blood and it is not at all easy to resolve, and here is the reason why from the perspective of one who has lived the argument.

Life in a mining area begins with an absolute given: people there are poor. When all you have to make a living is to dig up, blow up, chop down and drag off the very land you live on in order to prosper, then you are poor by any definition. The landowner may become wealthy for a while, but it is a transient thing because the landowner destroys the very thing—the land—that gives him prosperity. It lasts for only a few generations then the wealth is dissipated, spent, wasted and gone. The landowner can retreat to his land, but it will never bless him again because all that it had to prosper him has been taken and will never return.

The privileged would say the answer is obvious—let the landowner keep his pristine land and all will be well—but that argument is naïve and ignores the crushing effects of poverty. When you are poor enough, hungry enough, you will do what it takes to make life better. When you cannot afford health care for your children or shoes for their feet or clothes for your wife, then you will get on your knees and crawl down into the bowels of the earth and dig it and blast it for the rest of your life even if it kills you because that is the only choice you have and the land be damned.

Then along come environmentalists who live in cities or hipster communities with arts and crafts shows who wear Birkenstocks and knitted beanies and avoided military service and they lobby for laws to protect the land and the poor man and his little wife and children be damned.

And so the argument has always gone in eastern Kentucky, and it is the fool who fails to see it for what it is: a fight for survival. Now, give the miner a viable alternative with the same wages and he will jump on it in a heartbeat because no one wants to breathe in coal dust until their lungs are ruined or have a mine roof cave in on them and crush their bones, but until the better job comes along the poor man has got to go down into the mines and work.

The same goes for fracking. It is not so much about the land as it is good men and women wanting what so many other Americans already have—a nice house, a dependable automobile, good clothes and health care for their families. Give the men and women of the west a viable alternative and they will work elsewhere. As to the oil that lies underneath those ranches, the debate will continue to rage about the best way to get it out of the ground. Cheap gas at the pump will shut fracking down for a while, but it will be back when the price starts to rise and the debate will boil over again.

All of which means things are changing. Things are always changing and you need only take a trip around this great country of ours to realize just how much America is changing. My hometown is so white, so Republican and so Protestant that it is easy for someone who lives there and does not travel to assume that is the way the world really is. Hop on a bike, get in a car or jump on a plane and start seeing the rest of America, and it becomes readily apparent that the old *Leave It To Beaver,* white, middle-class America is fast becoming a thing of the past, and from my perspective that is a very good thing indeed.

The thing that makes America great is its cultural and racial diversity. We used to call America the "Great Melting Pot," but that is a term not often used in conservative circles today. It is because the white elite of this country have no desire for any melting to ever occur. Theirs is an enclave mentality, a fight to the last man, and I mean man, standing on the wall of that last bastion of white privilege—the segregated suburb and elite private educations for their children. To live like that is to miss all of the really good and kind and brilliant things that make this country great, and yet it goes on and on.

From my perspective, life is just way too short and the children of God way too precious to waste my energy denigrating someone because of their race, creed, color, ethnicity or sexual orientation. All it takes is to wake up one morning and realize your own body is eating itself alive to put things in perspective. Who gives a damn what race the oncologist is who is saving your life? Who gives a damn what sexual orientation the radiologist has who is lining up the machine to burn the cancer out of your body? The cancer patient who selects their physicians based upon their prejudice and bigotry is a fool.

I feel for the people in the fracking fight. It will be like the fight in the coal fields of my home. There will be powerful interests on both sides of the debate and the poor man will be crushed in the struggle unless he joins with other poor men and makes his voice heard.

My time with the large crane operators from Kentucky at the bar in Jonesboro demonstrates what men with skills can do. They will travel and work long and hard for their families back home in Kentucky. Learning the skill is the important thing.

I thought of the funny UPS driver I met earlier in the day. He is a Teamster who benefits from a great collective bargaining agreement and makes a good living for his family. He has what frackers and coal miners want, and he has it doing a job far less dangerous and complicated than the mining jobs that lie at the core of the mining debates. He has it because workers rose up and demanded a living wage.

Traveling on a motorcycle brings things up close and personal. You see, smell, taste and hear the very intimate individual communities that make up this country. America is such a complicated, diverse and opinionated society. We are many people, and yet we in the past have aspired to be one people. I hope we continue to do so.

My ride was winding down. Weather permitting, I would make it home tomorrow.

$\mathcal{D}$ay 11

$\mathcal{T}$rail's $\mathcal{E}$nd

-----Original Message-----

From: Brian House
Sent: Sunday, June 14, 2015 3:49 PM

I made it back home at dusk yesterday. I traveled 466 miles from Jonesboro, AR to my home in London. Altogether, I rode 4,371 miles on this 11-day trip. As you know, I cut the trip short by a week so I can attend my son's commissioning ceremony. There will be other trips, other destinations, but only one swearing in day.

I rode through familiar territory all day yesterday. I have duck-hunted in Arkansas in this area over the years so I know the places where I have hunted, but that is not at all to say I really knew the area. The towns are larger and the farms are more developed than it all appears when all you have on your mind is shooting ducks. I left Jonesboro early and rode east toward home and soon found myself back in rice fields and the wind that accompanies these vast areas of open ground. Thankfully, it didn't last long and I was able to enjoy the rising sun and the lush green crop fields of Arkansas before moving on over into Missouri which, in that area, is also heavily agricultural. Having been in the Southwest where water is a precious commodity and desert is the norm, the grass and crops in these Mississippi river valleys were almost neon green in their appearance. I crossed the Mississippi near Dyersburg, Tennessee.

I want to give the Mississippi River its due. There are other rivers in this country for sure. The Rio Grande, Missouri, Chattahoochee, Cumberland and the Ohio are waterways that are prominent in our literature and culture, but all of them lack the sheer mile-wide size and scale that gives the Mississippi its enduring grandeur. I have crossed her many times and every time I am in awe of her size. Now do that on a motorcycle at 65 mph in a crosswind on an elevated bridge and you come to respect the river even more.

Once I crossed the border into Kentucky, I was home. My wife is from Mayfield, so far western Kentucky has been home for me since 1977 even though London is my hometown. I rode to Mayfield and cruised by Susan's old street before riding over to the building which formerly housed the Merit Clothing Company. The Merit was for many decades a manufacturer of men's suits, both their label and for other more famous brands in the men's apparel industry. Susan's father was the Executive Vice President, Secretary and Treasurer of the Merit and worked there for 45 years. My first suits as a young lawyer came from the Merit and were manufactured in this building complex in downtown Mayfield. It seemed only right to get a picture of the old Merit with my GS since they both, in their own way, carried me some considerable distance from where I began two very different journeys in my life.

It was getting on toward the lunch hour as I left Mayfield. I knew where I wanted to eat and I hoped they would be open. I was in luck and found Belew's in Aurora, Kentucky doing brisk business. Belew's is a hamburger stand where the girls (yes, only girls) come out and take your order and then bring you your food. They even walk out to guys riding GS's and take their orders. When I arrived, the parking lot was packed with cars and a larger contingent of some sort of Jeep enthusiasts club, the kind where the owners throw tons of chrome and oversized tires on the outside and then fill the inside with leather and stereo equipment, it being their intention to strut in their Jeeps, but never really put them to the test. I had not been there for more than a couple of minutes when in roared a Harley contingent and they were typical in every conceivable Harley way. To a man they were all dressed alike, sporting black leathers, chains and bandanas. Just one or two helmets, and plenty of sleeveless t-shirts to, of course, show off all the ink on those biceps. I spoke to a few of them, but got no replies. I guess I just intimidated the hell out of them, what with me dressed like a great big banana in my yellow coat and yellow helmet.

Which brings me to Harley biker manners. When I was out west ALL riders waved to each other. We spoke at gas stations. We were interested in each other's gear. I don't know why, but once I was in Kentucky the waves stopped and the surly, "I wish I had been at the Waco biker shootout to be a badass" attitude blossomed. My theory on the good western manners has to do with geography. Things are so spread out in the western states, gas stations and repair assistance are so hard to find, that bikers know they need to rely on each other and are just glad to see someone who might be of assistance to them. Then come east where things are so concentrated and you are never more than five or 10 miles from gas, and it's suddenly easier to cop an attitude.

The lack of manners issue extended to the western Kentucky Jeep enthusiasts, or at least one of them. I had parked my bike in the parking lot just like everybody else. It was hot. I was tired. I had, as Mini-Hoss Cartwright had pointed out the day before, a genuine case of the sore-ass and I had been riding hard for three days. In short, just because I looked like a Chiquita banana did not mean I was not in the mood to be bothered. That's when a fancy Jeep redneck who was parked behind me stuck his baseball cap covered jug head out the window and said to me, "Hey buddy. Move your bike. I want to pull through there."

Now...my bike as loaded weighs about 650 pounds. I've just taken off my armor and helmet and ordered my hamburger.

I looked at Jeep boy and his woman and did what any proper southern gentleman would do. I said, "No."

And then I stood there.

Jeep boy got the message and moved on another way.

I wasn't about to let the parking lot encounter ruin my Belew's burger and chocolate shake. I thoroughly enjoyed them and then it was off toward Bowling Green where I would refuel and then hit the final leg for home.

I stopped at an IGA convenience store on the western side of BG to fill up. As I was doing so, a Harley comes roaring up. The rider was about my age. He too, like the other Harley guys, is invincible since he had no protective gear on unless you count the vest he was wearing over his skinny, chicken bones bare chest. He proceeded to fill his bike up. In a few moments, he peered around the island and spoke.

"Is that a BMW?"
"Yes," I replied.
"I thought so. My dad had one of those."

And so it goes. My relationship with Harley riders is a work-in-progress.

Fortunately, I did not have to speak with other Harley riders on the two-and-a-half-hour ride home from Bowling Green. I encountered one last brief rain shower in the final five minutes of my ride home and then it was over. I pulled into the driveway and there were Susan, Elliott and Sydney to greet me.

So here I am. The "I'm Still Here Tour 2015" is at its end. I traveled over 4,000 miles in 11 days and had a great time. I met interesting people and rode some really terrific roads. As you might expect, I have some more intimate personal reflections as a cancer survivor which I will share with some of you when the time is right. As to my friends in the world of BMW bikes, I'm going to do a follow-up piece on my experiences with equipment and the bike—what worked, what I liked and what I did not. I want to take a few days and reflect on that before I speak on the gear that got me through.

So, you may ask: "Was it worth it? Would you do it again?"

The answer to those questions is yes and yes. Look, riding a motorcycle is not for everyone. You have to WANT to do it, and if you want to get back alive you will follow up the want with a ton of preparation, practice and training. I did all of those and I used all of my training at some point on the trip. As to the worth of the thing, I will say that this was a physically demanding undertaking. It required stamina, physical strength in maneuvering a big bike around and a lot of coordination and self-confidence. Most of you have those things and take them for granted. Cancer patients do not. We are not what we once were or at least we worry that we are becoming less of who we were, that we are being diminished by the disease. In truth, age diminishes us all, but that is a slower progression than cancer can be if left untreated. I have never had a bad day since being diagnosed with prostate cancer, but the worry is always there, the fear of the thing is always floating around in the back of your mind somewhere. A trip like this served for me to assert my own existence on my terms, to say to the disease that came to kill me, "You may take my life, but you will never, ever take the living of a full life from me. I will live it up until the very end, disease be damned."

I hope to do other rides like this in the future. My new British friends invited me to do a next year's ride with them and I just may do it.

This blog started out as a way to just keep a few of you in the loop. It has evolved into something more as writing can and often does. Some of you know I write a lot. This little blog has given me an idea for another project. We'll see where it goes in the coming months.

Be safe and bless you all. I'll see you on the road...
Brian

***   ***   ***   ***   ***

This was my last day on the road. I got up early and rode out of Jonesboro before the heavy morning traffic began. I did not want my trip to end, but I wanted to get home in time to prepare for the trip to Nashville to see Elliott's swearing in.

By now, I was comfortable with my bike. I knew how it rode, how it cornered, how it accelerated and braked, how it just *felt* when I was on it and riding down the road. I was comfortable in the cockpit that existed behind my windscreen and the large black tank bag that sat against my chest. I used it frequently to lean against and rest while I rode. Living for hours and hours every day inside a helmet had become comfortable. I used earplugs to dampen the road noise. They did not block out all the sound, just the roar of the wind blowing by. Put it all together and it became a way of traveling that I enjoyed very much. I was as attentive on this last day as I was on the first, perhaps more so because some of that initial, giddy beginning of the trip excitement had been replaced by the relaxed immersion into the experience. I was comfortable with being on the road and finding whatever was out there and enjoying the experience. To now be on my last day when there was still so much out there to discover just left me wanting to do more of it and soon.

I had planned my route to take me through Mayfield, Kentucky. My wife was raised in Mayfield and is a proud graduate of Mayfield High School. She is the only member of her family to hold that honor. The rest of her siblings, being the obedient Catholic children they were raised to be, willingly went to St. Mary's Catholic High School 30 miles up the road in Paducah. Not my Susan, who was always a Protestant in disguise. She was a cheerleader for good old Mayfield High. I met her on campus at the University of Kentucky in the winter of 1977. It was love at first sight. My love affair with Susan led to my love of her family and western Kentucky. Her parents were gracious and loving to me from the first day I walked through their door. I was embraced with that deep southwestern Kentucky hospitality and I loved every minute of it. It was a transformative experience for me, smoothing some of the rough mountain edges off my personality and giving me insight into grace and kind manners.

Some young men find their father-in-law someone to be feared and avoided. It becomes a lifetime of dislike and separation. Not so for me. Susan's father and I hit it off from the very first time. We became and remained the closest of friends until he died of natural causes at the age of 94 in 2011. He was an irreplaceable mentor and supporter of mine. I learned from him to never waver in the support of family and to exert every resource and effort to make the family successful.

He was short. I was tall. He was Catholic. I was Protestant. He played cards. Me coming from a Baptist background, I had no idea how to play cards. He loved to hunt and so did I. We were both enthusiastic travelers. He had traveled far more widely than I. He fought in the Battle of the Bulge as a member of Patton's great army that marched across Europe and then came home to his wife who had waited patiently for his return. We consulted with each other as equals. He argued from our earliest days together that western Kentucky barbeque was the best in the state. He was right.

Susan and I spent many holidays and vacations at her parents' home in Mayfield. Sometimes we would go to Kentucky Lake and go out on the water in their boat, but I was just as happy to sit with Clarence in his den and talk. He had been a successful executive in the garment manufacturing industry and had a wealth of knowledge concerning production, supply logistics and labor relations. Even with all of that, he could discuss the most ordinary topics with anyone who walked through his door including me.

I rode into Mayfield and knew the first place I had to see was the old home place. Susan's family sold the home several years ago as her parents' health began to decline. Still, the two-story old brick on Fairlane Drive will always be my western Kentucky home so I had to see it before I left town.

I exited off the Purchase Parkway and rode the short distance to Fairlane Drive and made the familiar right turn that took me past the home with 212 on its mailbox. A new family lived there now and they had changed things. One of the maple trees had been cut down in the front yard and the trim of the house had been painted a different color. It was the same, but it wasn't. While I held great memories from that home, it would never be home again. New lives were being lived within its walls and they had their own path, their destiny, and it had nothing to do with me anymore.

I left Fairlane feeling a little melancholy, but there was another stop to make. I rode across town to the old Merit Suit Factory. Clarence worked there for 45 years, with his World War II service being the only interruption in his tenure. I parked the bike and walked around the now deserted plant. Apparel manufacturing jobs are all in China and other countries now. The men and women who made suits at this plant have long since died or moved onto other jobs. A plant that once employed thousands of highly skilled tailors and seamstresses in the flatlands of western Kentucky is now just a shell. It, like my father-in-law, has passed from the landscape that is contemporary Kentucky.

I took some pictures of the factory and made sure to get a

few of the window where Clarence's office had been. It was odd to look at the very place where he had spent so many years and would never be there again. As I stood there, I found myself smiling as I recalled the good times we had together, the trips we had taken, the bird hunts we had walking over the flat farms of Graves County. Those memories were mine forever.

I left Mayfield and rode into the lake country where Kentucky Lake and Lake Barkley are located. They were constructed as part of the massive Tennessee Valley Authority project to impound the Tennessee River by Kentucky Dam in 1944. Kentucky Lake is over 160,000 acres in size, with 2,064 miles of shoreline. It is the largest artificial lake by surface area in the United States and it is certainly a visual stunner. In places, it is over one-mile wide and, while not deep, its middle channel is deep enough for barges to regularly move through it.

For me, though, it will always be the place of my summer romance with Susan. We spent many happy days walking along the shoreline of the lake in 1977. We dined at the state park lodges and enjoyed our summer courtship with her family at their camping trailer by the lake.

A large body of water is a timeless thing. I got off my bike and walked down to the shoreline and listened to the water lapping up against the shore. Boats were running in every direction on the water. Families were enjoying their time along the banks of the lake just as I had done with my in-laws a lifetime ago. I felt a breeze blowing in off the lake like it had done since the impoundment first filled up in the 1940s. Who knows how many millions of people have stood on these shores and felt the comfort of these breezes? The lake winds outlast the people. I will stand here for a time and then be no more, but the lake will be here.

I rode by the old campsite where Clarence liked to keep his trailer at Sportsman's Resort. The resort was still packed with campers and very busy. Clarence's space was of course occupied by another trailer now, but the place looked much the same. I think he would have been pleased knowing that the business was continuing to prosper.

I grabbed a quick lunch at Belew's Drive-in at Aurora, Kentucky. Lunch was the obligatory cheeseburger and chocolate milkshake. To have ordered anything else there would have been sacrilege. The food was good as always. True, I did encounter some folks who did not understand how tired I was, but by this point in my trip I wasn't going to allow anything to ruin it.

I could do the ride from western Kentucky to London with my eyes closed. I have made that drive countless times over the years and yet, here I was riding in perfect weather and I started thinking to myself:

"Wouldn't it be terrible if I screwed this thing up and wrecked at the end?"

Fortunately, I did not. I made terrific time and was home by late afternoon.

I rode into my neighborhood feeling good. I had left here 11 days ago wondering if I could make this journey. Could I really ride all the way to New Mexico and back with no mishaps and be able to say I enjoyed the experience?

Well, I made it and it was a blast. I celebrated fighting back at cancer with every turn of the wheel of my bike. I learned I can still be among the living and enjoy my time here on earth. We are all leaving this place. It's up to each of us to chart our path, navigate the course and live life to the fullest.

I made that journey and came out of it a better man for having done so. I left my cocoon way behind, somewhere on the roads of Kansas that day as I cried my way through the Gypsum Hills. I learned to fly through life again.

Life is meant to be lived, to be embraced to the fullest no matter how much time you think you have left. Live every day. Let people know you love them. Take the time to hug babies and old folks and everyone in between. Be patient where patience is required and stand strong to defend those who cannot defend themselves.

Make life matter.

Finally, when you need a break, and we all do, get yourself a bike, take a chance and ride off into the sunset to find yourself.

It worked for me.

BCH
January 25, 2016

Chapter 18
I Made It!

First Lieutenant Elliott C. House, USAF taking the officer's oath
June 16, 2015
Air Force Recruiting Command
Nashville, Tennessee

Good Days Now

There are no bad days now.
Only good days.
Let it rain.
The sun is still there.
What has come
Has now gone.
Summer, winter, spring and fall
No matter.
I have fought the dragon
Felt his poker hot breath
And I have driven him into his lair.
I have walked with death and gasped from
its offal.
I am still here.
Mark the wounds and glimpse the healing.
I rise for another day
And the day after that.
They are all good days now.
I am still here.

Brian C. House
February 2016

Acknowledgements

The author would not be here without the concerted efforts of the following caring and so very talented physicians and institutions. You are God's instruments of healing and restoration. I owe all of you my life:

> Dr. Nancy V. Morris
> Dr. Alan P. Northington
> Dr. Bradley Bell
> Dr. William St. Clair
> Norton Hospital
> The University of Kentucky Markey Cancer Center

Special thanks to those faithful folks from my church, First Christian Church (Disciples of Christ), Middlesboro, Kentucky, who drove to Louisville to be with Susan and Sarah on the day of my surgery. You were my most precious church.

Special thanks to Bill and Christy Meader who drove from London to Louisville and sat with Susan on the day of my surgery. Bill and Christy, I will never forget you. I love you both.

Special thanks to my old friend and fellow minister the Rev. Dr. Michael S. Lee, who drove from Altavista, Virginia to pray with me and be with my family on the day of my surgery. You are my always irreplaceable friend.

Special thanks to old high school friends who wrote me, stopped by to visit, talked to me in parking lots and restaurants and let me know they cared—Judy Humfleet Faulconer, Pat Miller Bingham and Greg Mink.

Special thanks to Jo Nell Hays who has been my administrative assistant for 33 years. She is the sister I never had and was a prayer warrior during the darkest days of my diagnosis and recovery. God puts some people in your life and you just know they belong there. She is one of those.

Special thanks to my very good friend and bicycling buddy Dr. Michael Trosper. Mike got me back on the bicycle for a 40-mile ride as soon as the four-month post-operative moratorium on cycling was lifted by Dr. Bell. Mike continually boosted my spirits month after month, year after year as I made my way out of the cocoon to become the Butterfly Man. Others fell by the wayside, but Mike was always there.

Thanks to fellow lawyers Pierce Hamblin, Jeff Taylor, Otis Doan and Dan Partin. These men were always checking on me and offering up prayers on my behalf. It means so much to have men in your corner who care about you when the days are at their darkest. These were the men who hung with me.

Hats off to Bell Circuit Court Judge Bob Costanzo who issued an order directing cancer to leave me alone. All I can say Judge is it must have worked!

Special thanks and lots of hugs to my precious wife Susan who has tolerated my motorcycle madness just as she has tolerated my hunts in Africa and the mountains of Alaska. Baby, if there was an easier way to do this thing called life, it would not have been for me. I love you more than words can say.

Finally, but first above all others, I thank God for never abandoning me even in my darkest hour. He was always with me, abiding in me and giving me the strength to go forward. Exodus 14:14 became my battle verse. I needed only to be still, have faith in God and he would fight for me. He did and I am here. Praise be to God.

About Brian House

A modern day renaissance man, Brian House is a lawyer, ordained minister, writer, big game hunter, outdoorsman and traveler. His new book *The Butterfly Man* chronicles his motorcycle journey across America as he celebrates life after prostate cancer and reflects on survival, the people he met along the way and the places he discovered from Kentucky to New Mexico and parts in between. He is currently at work on a new novel. He resides in London, Kentucky.

More Books from...

Brand New Man: My Weight Loss Journey
Don McNay

Beans, Biscuits, Family & Friends: Life Stories
Bill Goodman

God's House Calls: Finding God Through My Patients
Dr. Jim Roach

Take More Naps (And 100 Other Life Lessons)
Dr. Keen Babbage

Life Lessons from a Dog Named Rudy
Dr. Keen Babbage

Death By Lottery: They hit the jackpot. They lost their lives.
Don McNay

The Art of Opinion Writing: Insider Secrets from Top Op-Ed Columnists
Suzette Martinez Standring

The Art of Column Writing: Insider Secrets from Art Buchwald, Dave Barry, Arianna Huffington, Pete Hamill and Other Great Columnists
Suzette Martinez Standring

Don McNay's Greatest Hits: Ten Years as an Award-Winning Columnist
Don McNay

Life Lessons from Cancer
Dr. Keen Babbage and Laura Babbage

Life Lessons from the Golf Course: The Quest for Spiritual Meaning, Psychological Understanding and Inner Peace through the Game of Golf
Clay Hamrick

Son of a Son of a Gambler: Joe McNay 80th Birthday Edition
Don McNay

Life Lessons from the Lottery: Protecting Your Money in a Scary World
Don McNay

Wealth Without Wall Street: A Main Street Guide to Making Money
Don McNay

Son of a Son of a Gambler: Winners, Losers and What to Do When You Win the Lottery
Don McNay

38932377R00140

Made in the USA
San Bernardino, CA
18 September 2016